SYMPTOM ANALYSIS

SYMPTOM ANALYSIS

A *Method of Brief Therapy*

M. Gerald Edelstien, M.D.

W. W. NORTON & COMPANY / NEW YORK / LONDON

First Edition

Library of Congress Cataloging–in–Publication Data

Edelstien, M. Gerald, 1928–
    Symptom analysis : a method of brief therapy / M. Gerald
Edelstien.
        p.   cm.
    Includes bibliographical references.

    1. Brief psychotherapy.   2. Psychotherapy, Brief.
    [1. Psychological Theory.]   I. Title.
    [DNLM: 1. Mental Disorders – therapy.   WM 420 E215s]
RC480.55.E34   1990   616.89'14 – dc20   89-70935

ISBN 0-393-70094-1

W. W. Norton & Company, Inc., 500 Fifth Avenue, New York, N.Y. 10110
W. W. Norton & Company, Ltd., 37 Great Russell Street, London WC1B 3NU

1 2 3 4 5 6 7 8 9 0

To Dot, with love

FOREWORD

MOST OF THE PSYCHOTHERAPY books I receive are tedious, un-readable, and unhelpful. My home and office are littered with books that I could contend with for only 10 or 20 pages. It's as if authors believe that the more difficult their prose and the more convoluted their ideas, the more profound they will be considered to be. This holds true not only for the more traditional analysts, but also for many of the practitioners of newer treatments, those who hold to double and triple binds and other Ericksonian machinations, the only effect of which is to put this reader into a deep sleep.

There are other books, of course, that are not so difficult to follow. But often they simply aren't useful to a practicing therapist. Very disturbing to me is that a great many books on psychotherapy em-phasize not results but rather correct technique. Is the therapist em-pathizing correctly, dealing with the transference in the right way, analyzing the right things, double-binding in the prescribed manner? How quickly we forget that the patient came in for help with some more or less specific problem and that progress in this regard is the only thing that matters. If it has been empirically demonstrated that doing a certain thing in a certain way produces superior results, then by all means let us learn to do it that way, but usually there is no such proof, only assertions that this way is the only correct way. The connection between doing things in this manner and obtaining the results the patient desires is left to the reader's imagination.

Something else that disturbs me about many of the books I've tried to read is that the authors do not emphasize brevity of treatment. Even some authors known for "brief" work now feel free to publish cases that go on for six months, a year, or even longer. Having learned in graduate school how to make therapy go on interminably, what I now want is to learn how to make it more efficient and shorter. I want to read people committed to the same goals.

In this wasteland of boring, useless manuals emphasizing all the wrong things (at least from my perspective), Gerry Edelstien's *Symptom Analysis* is a gem, all the things I value in a book on therapy. Written in clear English, with charm and wit, it helps considerably in simplifying the therapist's job.

One source of confusion to therapy students as well as veteran clinicians, and a cause of many boring books, is the huge number of theories explaining why people develop psychological problems. I believe Edelstien performs a valuable service by demonstrating that one therapy, a version of Freud's trauma theory, is really the explanation used by most schools of therapy, even though they manage to disguise it quite well. This helps simplify matters considerably. And I think his dismantling and unmasking of the unbelievably pedantic "ideas" of some of our grand theorists is nothing short of brilliant, reminiscent of the job C. Wright Mills once did on the "thought" of Talcott Parsons.

But perhaps what I like most about the book is the way he demonstrates how very brief therapy (in his case, an average of only six to eight sessions) is at least as effective as treatment lasting 10, 20, and even 50 times as long. This will not, of course, influence those therapists already committed to keeping their patients coming until the therapists' mortgages are paid off. But his clear examples may help persuade those who are not yet dedicated to such extravanganzas.

I think doing brief and effective therapy with the population Edelstien works with represents quite an achievement. Those of us in private practice have an easier time of it. A certain segment of the population, including some of the most difficult cases, is excluded because of our fees and also because we can be selective in whom we decide to treat. As will become clear in the book, Edelstien's cases run the gamut from simple adjustment problems to difficult psychoses and character disorders. Doing well with a significant percentage of this diverse group says something both about the man and the method.

Another thing I like about the book is the author's flexibility and careful attention to the patient's goals. Having talked to some of his former patients and watched him work a number of times, I know him to be a master clinician: truly able to listen to and understand his patients, open to what they need, and not bound by rigid ideologies and treatment techniques. He never forgets that the patient is there because he wants to sleep better, to be free of pain, be able to hold a job, get along better with his spouse or child, or something of the sort. Whatever it takes to achieve this goal is what he does.

This emphasis on concrete results is what allows him to be constructively eclectic: to use insight when that makes sense, to skip insight when it isn't needed, and to use techniques from a wide variety of schools.

One place his flexibility comes through is in his use of medications. Although most modern psychiatrists need no convincing about the benefits of drug therapy to some patients, psychologists and other nonmedical therapists often have been taught to avoid medications. This book may encourage them to rethink that position. In my own experience, far too many nonmedical therapists are unaware of the uses and advantages of drugs and don't even consider them. I have seen scores of patients with serious depression (in some cases even manic-depression), psychoses, and other problems who spent years in therapy to no avail and were not even informed about the drug options. My experience is like Edelstien's. While drugs are by no means a panacea and have problems of their own, they certainly have a place in the treatment of many of the problems we see in clinics and private practices.

One concern I have about *Symptom Analysis* is that some readers may be put off by Edelstien's extensive use of hypnosis, a technique that is a turn-off to many therapists. Having seen him do his kind of hypnosis many times (which, it should be said, is straightforward and includes very little of the mumbo-jumbo used by many hypnotherapists), and having talked to some of the patients he did it with, I think it's important not to get sidetracked by this issue. He uses hypnosis simply because it works well for him. And, as he points out in the book, other techniques work just as well. Besides, hypnosis isn't exactly a technique. It's more like a way of relating to patients and its use doesn't preclude the use of any other technique, everything from free association to systematic desensitization.

This is an important book because it gives many examples of how our thinking about therapy, and our therapy practice, can be made simpler (but not simple-minded), effective, and brief. It is one of only a handful of therapy books I've read in the last few years that I learned from. Edelstien is a master clinician and teacher; being in his company, even if only on paper, is a comforting and enlightening experience. *Symptom Analysis* is a book I recommend without hesitation to those who actually think about what they're doing rather than merely following approaches they once were taught, and to all who are concerned with making their therapy shorter and more helpful.

Bernie Zilbergeld, Ph.D.
Oakland, California
Author of *Male Sexuality* and *Mind Power*

CONTENTS

ACKNOWLEDGMENTS

I WISH TO THANK Marcia Cuñha, M.S.W., for her generous help with the research. Her labors saved many hours of my own. My thanks to Judith Fabian, Ph.D., Gerry Manus, Ph.D., Paul Palmbaum, M.D., George Ponomareff, M.D., and especially Bernie Zilbergeld, Ph.D., for their helpful comments and criticisms. Their labors added many hours to my own. Finally, I wish to thank Susan Barrows, the finest editor I've ever had. The fact that she's the only editor I've ever had doesn't matter. Each time I've worked with her has been a pleasure and an education.

INTRODUCTION

FREUD (1928) STATED that the interpretation of dreams is the royal road to the unconscious. If that statement does not stand up well to scientific scrutiny, at least it is ironically prophetic. Today, if one chooses to follow that road, it can cost a king's ransom to reach the destination.

Royal though it may be, this road is neither swift nor certain. It contains numerous false starts, detours, and dead ends because the roadside markers, which are the symbols in the dream, are woefully inconsistent. Freud himself said. "At times a cigar is only a cigar," but in practice that seems to apply only when the therapist dreams of one. When the patient dreams of a cigar it is usually interpreted as a blatant phallic symbol. A house may represent, among other things, the body of the dreamer or his brain, with significant memories residing in each room. Some therapists, remembering Freud's comment about the cigar and utilizing bold imagination, may believe that the house, at times, may represent only a house; other therapists, because they have no imagination at all, with *always* believe that a house represents only a house.

Of course, the "true" interpretation of dream symbols lies in the context of the dream, what is transpiring in therapy (including the stage of the transference), what is going on in the patient's current life, and what his associations are to the present, the past, and even the future. This would all be very well if there were then some consistency to the interpretations, but I have never heard a group of therapists discuss a dream and initially all come to the same conclusion about its meaning. Perhaps, after prolonged discussion, they will come to the same conclusion, but what does this say about what goes on in the therapist's office, where there is no group of colleagues to participate in such a discussion? It means, perhaps, that at times the patient may not receive the "correct" interpretation. In other words, once the road has been traveled, there is little certainty as to what destination has been reached.

If the wrong interpretation has been reached, the therapist, unaware of his error, may do one of two things. He may work with the patient's "resistance" to the interpretation, or he may travel further afield, hand in hand with the patient, who, unaware of his own error, accepts the interpretation. The patient, as good patients often do, may even elaborate on the interpretation.

I hope that in this book I can demonstrate that, *rather than using the interpretation of dreams as a royal road to the unconscious, we can use the interpretation of symptoms as a freeway to the unconscious, and that methods of short-term therapy provide excellent vehicles for the journey.* Admittedly, the journey will not be as extravagantly scenic as one would find on the royal road, but it will be faster and more direct. This I believe is important, not only for the welfare of the patients who come to see us, but also for the welfare of our profession. In this day of increasing fiscal restraints, our best hope of remaining a viable profession is for us to be able to demonstrate that good therapy can be done quickly and in a relatively cost-effective way.

This is not a popular idea among those whose entire experience has been devoted to doing long-term therapy, for it means the abandonment of a style of practice that has become familiar and comfortable, and also requires the questioning of theories that have long been accorded more value than they might deserve. It further requires a flexibility and innovativeness that many therapists do not possess.

This book is being written for those therapists who do have flexibility of ideas and of techniques, and for the benefit of their patients.

Therapists' resistance to change was illustrated nicely when I expressed some of my ideas in the newsletter of a local professional society. My thoughts were that we needed to adapt to changing times and intensify our efforts to learn and improve methods of short-term therapy. One of the offended long-term therapists responded that short-term therapy is like having a mechanized tomato picker plucking green tomatoes from the vine without allowing them ample time to ripen and develop their full flavor and texture. I do not see any persuasive logic in comparing psychotherapy to the picking of tomatoes, but if such an analogy were to be used, it may be more accurate to think of it in these terms: When the tomato is ripe, that is, when the patient decides to enter therapy, it is far better to become active and pick the fruit quickly than to sit contemplatively, interpreting the stages of its development and waiting until it decides to drop off the vine by itself.

To "pick the fruit quickly," we can *analyze the symptoms* that brought the patient into therapy. Symptom analysis means simply that we learn when the symptoms developed, the circumstances that led to their development, the feelings that those circumstances evoked, and perhaps most importantly, the ways in which those symptoms may have served some useful purpose to the patient.

I consider the analysis of symptoms to be an insight-oriented therapy, for it gives the patient "insight" into what has caused his problems. If the therapy is successful, it also permits "insight" into why the symptoms have been maintained and what can be done to stop them.

Patients do not enter therapy because of transference reactions to the therapist. I hope that this book will raise serious questions about the necessity of letting a transference neurosis develop so it can be analyzed and resolved, for such a process leads to long-term therapy.

Patients do not enter therapy because of resistance to therapy. Too much focus on resistance leads to long-term therapy. Patients enter therapy because of *symptoms*. Perhaps this book will demonstrate that rigorous focus on those symptoms leads to therapy that is brief and to benefits that are long lasting.

To better understand when and where symptom analysis is appropriate, I have organized the various disorders listed in *DSM-III* according to what I believe to be the primary etiology of those disorders. This seems reasonable, since nonpsychiatric disorders are grouped in such a way. For example, in diseases of the brain and other organ systems, there will be groupings based upon whether the diseases are caused by tumor, trauma, metabolic errors, circulatory disturbances, etc. Etiological groupings of the psychiatric disorders are, however, far from satisfactory, for we know so little about the etiology of most of them. Presumably most, if not all, of them represent a complex interplay of biological and psychological factors, making such classifications even more precarious.

There will therefore be much room for justifiable criticism of my groupings. I have made them nonetheless *because they may serve as useful guidelines to treatment planning*. The groups that I use are:

1. *Psychological disorders with obscure origins.* By "obscure origins" I mean that the source of the difficulty is not readily apparent. Others would express the same idea by saying that repression has occurred, so that the source of the difficulty is now "unconscious." For these, I generally attempt insight-oriented therapy. I would include in this list some phobias (others have an obvious origin), somatization disorder, conversion disorder, psychogenic pain disorder, hypochondriasis, psychogenic amnesia, psychogenic fugue, multiple personality disorder, depersonalization (if not caused by drugs or panic disorder), some of the psychosexual dysfunctions, ego-dystonic homosexuality, psychological factors affecting physical conditions, and many of the personality disorders (at least the milder ones).

2. *Psychological disorders with obvious origins.* Instead of using "obvious origins," others would say "conscious" or "precon-

scious." Here I would include some of the phobias, almost all of the adjustment disorders, and post-traumatic stress syndromes (certainly the acute and chronic variations; I suspect the delayed ones may have more of an organic aspect than we have yet discovered).

3. *Organic disorders*. Here I'm not speaking of the usual dementias, organic brain syndromes, etc., but of such problems as substance use disorders, schizophrenic disorders, the major affective disorders, some of the anxiety disorders (including panic disorder, perhaps generalized anxiety disorder, and at least the more severe cases of obsessive-compulsive disorder), at least some of the psychosexual disorders, and at least some of the disorders of impulse control, like intermittent explosive personality disorder.

For the researcher there are a variety of reasons that accurate diagnoses are important. These include the need to study the etiology, prevalence, morbidity, and natural courses of the disease, and to compare the relative efficacy of different treatment modalities. To the clinician, however, the primary importance of a diagnosis is to determine the type of treatment that he will use, and for me, at least, these groupings help with that task.

Let me repeat: I know that there will be much disagreement about these classifications, for they cannot possibly be as distinct as I have made them. There must be a complex interplay between the organic and psychological factors in each of them. Without a certain minimal amount of biological activity going on, the patient would have minimal amounts of responsiveness, and his emotional reactions would become as restricted as those of a therapist doing traditional long-term therapy. With even less biological activity, he would be brain dead or plain dead, and if there were any emotional responses at all, no one could detect them. (A few decades later, though, some past lives regression therapist might claim that he could.) So, acknowledging again that these divisions are not exact but do provide a focus for therapeutic interventions, I will try to demonstrate how they become useful in practice.

Before doing so, however, perhaps I should briefly describe the setting of my practice and the patient population that I see, since both were influential in my thinking.

After eleven years of a private psychiatric practice in Berkeley, California, I joined an HMO on a full-time basis in 1980. I hoped that such a setting would enable me to test and further develop some of the ideas I had already formulated about short-term therapy. I was also motivated by my expectation that fee-for-service psychiatry would become less palatable as the whole system of health care funding went through extensive changes. My hope and my expectation were both realized.

Members of the Kaiser Health Plan are entitled to a maximum of 20 psychiatric visits a year, at fees ranging from one to 20 dollars per visit. Many of the members are also able to receive medications for only one dollar per prescription. Because of this availability of affordable services, we see many patients who probably would not seek help if it were more expensive for them to do so. Few, however, come for frivolous reasons.

About 20% of those who call for an initial appointment never show up. We do not know how often that's a matter of resistance or a matter of having solved some acute problem on their own. This 20% failure rate remains pretty consistent and appears to be independent of the waiting period, be it six weeks or 24 hours.

Few patients require the full 20 visits. For my patients, therapy is terminated by mutual agreement in an average of four to five visits, although in rare instances I might see a patient for as many as 30 visits in the course of two fiscal years.

Last year, which was probably pretty typical, I took in 195 patients for individual therapy, and although I had offered another 50 intakes, those patients did not keep their appointments. In addition to the individual therapy patients, I saw 25–30 new patients per month in the two crisis groups that I co-lead, was called upon six to twelve times a day to offer consultations (usually brief ones, and mostly concerning medications) to the seven non-M.D. therapists on our adult treatment team, and did about 25 follow-up medication visits (15 minutes each) per week.

All in all, then, I have the opportunity to see hundreds of new patients each year, providing crisis intervention, insight-oriented therapy, supportive therapy, and psychopharmacology. The setting has been excellent for shaping and refining my ideas, although there may be debate about the excellence of the ideas that were so refined.

Demographically, in rough figures, the patients are female in a 2 : 1 ratio: 64% are married, 23% single, and 11% separated/divorced. Their ages range from 17 into the 70's (younger patients are seen by our child treatment team); 80% are between 21 and 50, with the largest single grouping, 30%, in the 21–30 year spread. Educationally, 51% have had at least some college education, including 19% who have done postgraduate work. Their employment status includes 51% with professional or white collar jobs and 21% with blue collar jobs; most of the others are students, housewives, or retirees. Very few are unemployed.

Diagnostically the patients I've seen individually have had: adjustment disorders, 39%; depression, 24%; personality disorders, 10%. Only 4% were given a diagnosis of schizophrenia or manic-depressive disorder. These figures underestimate the number of depressions and anxiety disorders, including panic disorders, that come to our clinic, for a high percentage of these are referred directly to our crisis groups, so that we might evaluate them and commence treatment as quickly as possible. Substance abuse disorders are not seen in our clinic for individual therapy, but are referred to a substance abuse program at one of our neighboring facilities.

Of the patients that I see, approximately 15–20% are considered appropriate for symptom analysis. This determination is made almost exclusively on whether or not I consider them to have a problem that fits into the category of "psychological disorders with obscure origins." I do not use other exclusionary criteria, for, although my success rate might be higher if I did, I believe the patients deserve an opportunity to give it a try.

SYMPTOM
ANALYSIS

I | *T*HEORIES AND *T*HERAPIES

1 | Theories about the Origins of Psychiatric Symptoms

ANY THOUGHTFUL therapist should have serious questions about the validity of any of the theories currently available to explain the origins of psychiatric symptoms. It has been estimated that there are 200 to 400 different types of psychotherapy. I have not seen estimates on how many different theories exist, but the number must be large to support so many different kinds of therapy. Any honest therapist will admit that there is precious little scientific evidence to prove any of these theories and that, although some are quite contradictory to others, all seem to work some of the time, and none works all of the time. Despite the uncertainty that should exist, some therapists still believe as fervently in their particular theories as some religious zealots believe that theirs is the only true religion among the hundreds of others that are equally dear to other zealots.

To support his belief in one theory or another, the therapist has at least three maneuvers available, none of which can stand up to close scrutiny.

First, he can quote authority. *Ad hominem* arguments, however, cannot be considered reliable, for ultimately the originator of the theory can quote only himself, and unless he can demonstrate rather convincingly that he received the word from God, it should not be considered heresy to question any statements advanced by that authority.

Second, he can claim that the information that the patient reveals in the course of therapy supports his theory. This is no proof at all, for no matter what theory the therapist is using, his patients will offer information to support that theory. I believe this to be true across the whole spectrum of therapies, including what might be considered two extremes, classical Freudian psychoanalysis and past lives regression therapy.

I have heard or read cases presented by analysts, past lives regression therapists, and therapists of other theoretical persuasions. Each of them has reported information from his or her patients that coincided with that therapist's particular theoretical beliefs. Anyone who has had the adventure of listening to therapists from differing schools almost certainly has made the same observation.

Judd Marmor's observations of this phenomenon have been cited by Grunbaum (1984). He observed that a "free-associating" patient invariable produces "data" that corroborate his therapist's particular school of thought, be it classic Freudian, Jungian, Kleinian, or whatever.

Gustafson (1986) adds to this observation:

> Each distinction [by "distinction" Gustafson is referring to opposing currents in the patient's life] allows the patient and therapist to tell a class of related stories. For Malan, the stories are about patients who are devoted to their duty, narrowly, until the therapist helps them discover their opposite true feelings. For Mann, the stories are of patients who have struggled so long and hard to be something worthwhile, but, in spite of their best efforts, they find themselves back in pain. For Sifenos, the stories are of patients who pretend to be children sneaking around with sexual interests, because they are afraid to own up to their powerful, adult, sexual demands. For Davanloo, the stories are of patients who sit passively behind walls of vagueness, until the wall is destroyed by the therapist, whereupon the patient has a breakthrough into true feeling. Obviously, it is possible to draw points

of overlap between these four classes of stories, but it is remarkable how each of these four therapists generates his own class of story over and over again. (p. 133)

Patients even present dreams that coincide with their therapists' particular theoretical bent. Freudian patients present Freudian dreams; Jungian patients, Jungian dreams; existential patients, existential dreams.

We have an intellectual obligation to wonder what this means. Does it mean that we overtly, or somehow covertly, suggest to our patients what they should tell us? Does it mean that we selectively extract from our patients' reports only that which we wish to hear? Does it mean that we selectively interpret (or unwittingly distort) what patients tell us so we can make it fit into our own scheme of things? Does it mean that patients select us because they surmise that we'll be interested in the sort of information that they have a penchant for revealing? We cannot answer any of those questions yet, although I suspect that each of those possibilities occurs in varying proportions. Whatever the answers may be, it should be clear that we cannot use our patients' revelations as proof of our theories.

Not all patients, of course, immediately reveal what their therapists expect to hear. What does the therapist do then? If the patient's information is contrary to the therapist's expectations, s/he's unlikely to consider the possibility that the theory is at fault. Instead, s/he will believe that the patient is displaying a "resistance," even though there may be no evidence to support that claim other than the circular argument that if the patient disagrees with an interpretation or doesn't reveal what the therapist expected to hear, then that is sufficient proof of a resistance being present.

If another therapist disagrees with the first therapist's interpretation or theoretical formulation, that may also be labeled a resistance, if the two therapists belong to different theoretical schools. If they belong to the same school, it may be considered ignorance, technical error, or superior judgment, depending upon the relative esteem one holds for the other. The very fact that there was disagreement about the interpretation, though, means that at least one, and conceivably both, therapists were in error. If the patient, however, had disagreed with either one during a session, it is far more likely that this would be considered a sign of resistance rather than of error on the therapist's part.

If the "resistant" patient remains in therapy and later reveals the information that the therapist had expected to hear earlier, then the therapist will use this as "proof" of an earlier resistance. A more objective observer, however, might be inclined to say that this is merely a delayed example of the fact that patients will (eventually) produce data that supports their therapist's theory. That objective observer, if afflicted with a touch of cynicism, might even believe that the eventual delivery of the "correct" data was actually the result of the therapist's repeated, subtle (or not so subtle) suggestions. After all, any interpretation is really a suggestion that something is true, and when the same interpretation is made repeatedly, patients may eventually begin to believe it.

Interestingly, when a therapist who has worked with one theory reads or hears about a new one and starts working with it, he immediately finds that now his patients are giving data to support that newer theory. His former colleagues will still be getting data to support the older one.

Less often, the therapist's clinical observations do raise questions about his old theory, and then he proceeds to find or invent a new one himself. Did Kernberg ever write about a lack of data to support the older theories he worked with before inventing his own? He obviously now finds different data to support his newer theories.

The third strategy that a therapist has for "proving" the validity of his theory is the display of successful cases. Even if he's not lying about his successes (and such a travesty is not without precedent), his successes prove nothing about his theory. As has been mentioned earlier, those therapists with very different theories are also claiming successes, and all indications are that they're having them in equal proportions.

It's quite possible that Freud was the first psychotherapist to claim that his successes proved the validity of his theories. It's also possible that he was the first to lie about this. Crews (1986, pp. 59–60) says:

> If Freud had permanently removed a single neurosis, no doubt he would have told us about the case in detail. But the pro-Freudian researchers Seymour Fisher and Roger P. Greenberg have regretfully concluded that nearly all of Freud's substantially described cases were manifest failures. . . . And often Freud simply misrepresented therapeutic outcomes . . . as, for example, in reporting the eighteen successfully completed cases that underlay "The Aetiology of Hysteria" (1896). In other papers of the period he never mentioned more than thirteen cases, and shortly after delivering that paper he complained to Fliess, "I get no new cases for treatment, and – not one of the old ones is finished yet" (Freud, 1954, pp. 162–63). Even two years later he had yet to mention a successful termination; on the contrary, he confided that his cases were still "doing rather badly" (Freud 1954, p. 245).
>
> In 1906 Freud confided to Jung that "It is not possible to explain anything to a hostile public; accordingly I have kept certain things that might be said concerning the limits of the therapy and its mechanism to myself. . . . " Only toward the end of his career, when his undeserved reputation as a healer was secure, did he begin confessing from time to time that he had "never been a therapeutic enthusiast" . . . and that he had not found a reliable remedy for neurosis at all. . . . Yet he did not feel prompted by that momentous admission to withdraw any of the theoretical claims he had rested on his previous untruths about therapeutic triumph.

There are good reasons to be dubious about *ad hominem* arguments and proofs based upon claimed successes.

Despite their weaknesses, it is inevitable that we have theories. Since humans first had the capacity to think, they started developing theories to help them deal with the unknown. In years past, it was very easy to develop a theory: if something good or bad happened, it could be attributed to the actions of a god or a demon. Now that we have become more sophisticated, we have the ability to develop more sophisticated theories. But that doesn't imply that they're necessarily more reliable.

A theory is a valuable tool for scientific progress. It serves as a reference point for examining just what causes might lead to just what effects. It becomes a hindrance to progress, however, when one person announces a theory and followers soon accept it as a fact, looking only for evidence to support it and denying any evidence that discredits it. That, I believe, has led to much of what is wrong in our profession today.

I personally believe that it's useful to employ one theory or another when doing psychotherapy. The theory provides direction for the therapist as s/he makes interventions, and it provides a rationale for the patient to make some changes. A theory, then, can serve a very important function, even when it's wrong. Any therapist using a theory, however, should choose one that is unlikely to do too much harm to innocent people, as some of them have done in the past, and as some may still be doing.

As an example of the former, we can look at the theory of the "refrigerator mother" as an explanation for childhood autism—an explanation that left many a mother with a terrible burden of guilt. As an example of the latter, I would consider past lives regression therapy. Here, the hypnotized patient is "regressed" to some "prior life experience" and comes out of the trance thoroughly convinced that the experiences were real. Although this could make the patient a local celebrity in California, it could lead to social ostracism if s/he ever moved to Kansas.

Therapists should also recognize that if they are gullible enough to accept any theory, their fellow believers may admire this act of blind faith, but more objective observers will think of them less kindly.

For many years we've had available to us an unpretentious little theory that can be used to understand and relieve symptoms with relative ease. It's extremely useful, even if it, too, is proven to be wrong. Let's call it *the trauma theory*.

2 | THE TRAUMA THEORY

The patient experienced a traumatic incident (or series of traumatic incidents) that caused some very painful feelings. In an effort to protect himself/ herself from experiencing those painful feelings again, s/he adopted certain new behaviors, feelings, or attitudes. If those adaptive changes create problems, s/he is said to have symptoms.

THAT'S ALL THERE IS to it, although there is a corollary that I'll mention later.

An extremely simple case example would be: A man is driving along the freeway and becomes involved in a bad accident. He assuredly would experience painful feelings. There would be physical pain in some instances, and there would almost always be emotional pain as well. Those painful feelings might include: anger, if he believed the other driver to be at fault; guilt, if he believed himself at fault; and fear, no matter who was at fault.

If the combined feelings were so painful that he experienced a critical need to prevent their recurrence, there is no way he could avoid that danger more effectively than by refusing to drive on the freeway again. This refusal would protect him from the pain of having another accident on the freeway, but it would constrict his life, and so we would say that he had a symptom, i.e., a freeway phobia.

We know that only a small percentage of people who have accidents develop a driving phobia afterwards, and why some do and others do not is a question we cannot answer as yet. However, since therapists have an incurable need to develop theories for explaining any aspect of human behavior that we know little about, we do have theories on that subject.

There are those who might say that the patient's damaged automobile, undoubtedly a phallic extension of himself, has reawakened castration fears that were never adequately resolved, and so an analysis of those castration fears is in order. Others might say that his feeling of utter helplessness, or his expulsion from the car, or his extraction from it reawakened unresolved issues surrounding his birth, so he must be regressed to that traumatic experience. I presume others would contend that he had been involved in a chariot accident on the Appian Way, and had to reexplore one of his former lives as an ancient Roman traffic statistic.

Dr. Edith Fiore, for example, has recently stated (1988) that if a patient has acrophobia, it's because he died in a fall in some prior life. If he has a fear of water, it's because he had drowned, etc.

There are others who would contend that concurrent problems of the day had created an emotional state which made the patient vulnerable to symptom development at the time of the accident. There are those who would suspect that his catecholamine metabolism caused an abnormally strong response at the time of the accident, and merely imagining driving again restimulates that response, causing an inordinate amount of anxiety.

I would be inclined to say that I don't know, and that it's unfortunate that others aren't always equally willing to admit a lack of certainty.

Although neither I nor the other therapists know why the symptom developed in this particular patient, that would not prevent any of us from trying to treat the patient, each according to his or her own favorite theory, and each of us having approximately the same chance for success. The trauma theory, however, may enable the achievement of that success more quickly than some of the others.

The trauma theory that I have presented is certainly not original. As a matter of fact, it's been proposed before by a variety of authors. Unfortunately, those authors have the talent of saying the same thing in such a complicated and convoluted style that they disguise the fact that this is all that they're saying. To camouflage it even further, they introduce new terminology and/or become very specific about the types of traumatic events that they believe each patient will have experienced.

Some say the trauma is the reemergence of infantile drives and wishes: others say it's the anxiety of separation; others, the humiliation and anger when parents did not adequately admire childhood achievements. Undoubtedly, each of these specifics do apply to some individual patients, but I seriously question the justification for such specificity for all patients who happen to have the same symptom.

The whole process of camouflaging the trauma theory is most regrettable, for it can lead unwary readers into believing that they have come across some great new truth from some great new authority, when, in fact, they are merely being led away from seeing clearly what is being done. It's possible that these authorities deliberately tried to make names for themselves by paraphrasing some predecessor. I prefer to believe that their thinking, and therefore their writings, were so painfully complicated that they had no realization that this is what they were doing.

Freud probably was the first to propose the trauma theory. I paraphrased it slightly. It was originally called his theory of traumatic neurosis, but since *DSM-III* has eliminated the term "neurosis," his theory has been given a more modern name.

After Freud had talked to a number of patients and reached the conclusion that the traumas were all of a sexual nature, his theory became known as the seduction theory. Still later, he decided that the seductions were fantasies, not real, and he came up with the concept of infantile drives and wishes, etc. As he pursued his belief that these frightening offspring of the id were responsible for emotional trauma, his seduction theory evolved into what is now known as psychoanalysis.

One wonders if all evolution is really a benefit to the species?

Now, if we can look at complex psychoanalytic formulations, we can see that the trauma theory remains intact, as long as we do not let the complexities distract us too badly. Let's use as the first example Freud's case of Little Hans. (Freud, 1909)

In this case a young child was psychoanalyzed by his father to treat a phobia of horses. We are told that Hans had forbidden instinctual strivings in that he wanted to seduce his mother and wanted his father dead so that he, Hans, could have her all to himself. Because he also loved his father, he could not bear the guilty feelings of wanting to kill him, so he "projected" these feelings in such a way that it was his father who wanted to harm Hans. Thus, he became afraid of his father's retaliation via castration, but that fear was too intolerable, so he "displaced" that fear to horses that might bite him.

Let us assume, briefly, that this fanciful explanation were true. The trauma theory would explain his phobia like this: Hans had a traumatic experience, i.e., he experienced the emergence of forbidden instinctual strivings. That emergence caused painful feelings. In order to avoid having those feelings again, he developed a phobia of horses.

This is obviously too brief a summary to make any rational sense, particularly since we are compelled to include Freud's idea of the instinctual strivings, as well as mechanisms of defense like projection and displacement. Therefore, let's break it into smaller steps.

Hans experienced an initial traumatic event: he recognized instinctual strivings to have his mother to himself by means of eliminating his father. This caused painful feelings of guilt. He attempted to protect himself from that guilt by projecting the hostile impulses onto his father. This attempt became a second traumatic event, for the belief that his father wished to harm him produced painful feelings of fear. He attempted to protect himself from that fear by displacing the father's hostile impulses onto the horses. This became a third traumatic event, producing the fear that horses would harm him. To protect himself from that fear, he avoided them.

As a matter of record, Hans had actually been frightened by a falling horse shortly before his phobia developed. It seems reasonable to believe that this was the real reason for his fear of them.

This simple explanation seems like common sense to me, and perhaps to a few of you, but since common sense doesn't always carry much weight in this, my chosen profession, and since it's not always right, I'll quote briefly from Budman and Gurman (1988, p. 78).

> Those who are robbed tend to be overly frightened of future robberies (Stinchcombe et al., 1980). Rape victims develop great fears that this event will happen again (Burgess and Holmstrom, 1974). Those who have recovered from severe medical illnesses such as cancer (Burdick, 1975) are more likely than others to overinterpret discomfort and normal symptomatology as indicating a recurrence of their disease process (Kellner, 1985).

Although I did not find a study specifically describing what happens to the victims of falling horses, it's reasonable to expect that maybe they follow a similar pattern.

But if we're to consider such a mundane explanation for the phobia, what are we to do with an explanation as imaginative as the one Freud offered? We can look for proof to confirm his explanation. There is no proof, other than the material that Hans had to offer (and often even that was first supplied by his father, the therapist, and then parrotted by Little Hans). I hope that this type of proof is no longer considered adequate.

What proof is there for the mundane explanation? No more than there is for the fancier one. Which one, then, are we to believe? The most rigorous answer can only be "neither." But since a theory is useful, even if wrong, the trauma theory, without the elaborations about forbidden instinctual strivings, would permit a less elaborate therapy that would certainly be briefer and probably every bit as effective as the analytic one.

Let us not concentrate exclusively on Freud, for, after all, he was the first analyst and had no access to the combined experience and prolific writings of others. What do more modern analysts have to say? One could read Kernberg. I don't, because the gains are just not worth the effort involved. I do read about Kernberg, though, and will quote Adler (1986). I hope readers will make the effort of reading this passage quickly, even if they find it as painful as I do.

> Kernberg stresses the narcissistic personality disorder patient's need for a position of self-sufficiency as a central part of the disorder, and the pathological internal object relations that Kernberg describes allow the patient to feel self-sufficient; under these circumstances he does not have to acknowledge the separate existence of the other person and his feelings of helplessness, envy, and rage about that person. A central aspect of Kernberg's formulation is that the narcissistic patient cannot tolerate his envy and rage toward the person with whom he is involved. His pathological internal world allows him to deny his needs, envy, and rage which would be present in a relationship with that person, who is separate from him and whom he cannot control. Rage and devaluation also protect the patient from acknowledging his intense needs for the other person. Of course, he pays a huge price for such defensive structure . . .
>
> Kernberg emphasizes the importance of the pathological grandiose self in narcissistic personality disorder (made up of the ideal self, real self, and ideal object). This grandiose self is projected onto the other person, who can then be seen as omnipotent and someone to be idealized. Thus, the idealization in Kernberg's formulation is viewed as defensive—a projection of the patient's own pathological grandiosity. *It can serve to protect the patient against his own early self-devaluation and helplessness and the acknowledgment of the other person's separateness.* (italics mine)

This is an excellent example of how the trauma theory can become so convoluted that it's unrecognizable. I believe that the author could have said, "Something happened (not specified) that caused the patient to devalue himself. This caused intolerably painful feelings of helplessness, envy and rage in regard to the other person. To protect himself from those painful feelings he developed a grandiose view of himself, which he also projects upon the other person in a relationship. This self-devaluation additionally created another painful feeling, an intense need for the other person. Rage toward and devaluation of the other person protect the patient from feeling this intense need."

This sounds more comprehensible to me; it is merely a restatement of the trauma theory plus elaboration about the specific painful feelings and the symptoms employed to prevent their recurrence.

Adler also writes about Kohut's views of the narcissistic personality disorder. While the language remains tedious, it is worth examining closely to see how that which sounds so profound when stated in such pompous terms actually expresses very little that we do not already know. The paragraphing is mine, and following Adler's words are my attempts to translate this into English. (p. 432)

> . . . a child requires parents who can provide phase-appropriate "mirroring" as well as be available as figures to be idealized, so that the child can "merge" with the soothing qualities of the idealized parent. Mirroring consists of the parents' recognizing the emerging aspects of the child's self and responding appropriately to them. In normal development, Kohut described mirroring as the "gleam in the mother's eye" when she responds to the child's exhibitionistic displays. [*Translation*: Children need parents who are good role models and who express their pleasure as the child shows off his new accomplishments.]
>
> When appropriate, the parent is sensitive to the child's grandiose self and his need to have this emerging self confirmed. [*Translation*: The parent is sensitive to the child's need for attention.]
>
> The grandiose self of the child is gradually transformed into the healthy ambitions of the adult through parental responses that take into account the phase-appropriate needs, capacities, and vulnerabilities of the child. [*Translation*: The parents gradually teach the child to become less self-centered.]
>
> In addition, the child develops aspects of his self by taking in functions he needs from the idealized self-object through the process of transmuting internalization, a process involving the internalization of functions that the other person has and that the child (or patient) needs. [*Translation*: The child learns from the parents how to deal with the problems of everyday life.]
>
> Implied in the importance of intense self-object needs is the tenuous self-cohesiveness of the narcissistic personality disorder patient. When the self-object disappoints the patient through some "empathic failure," i.e., failure to understand or respond in the way the patient may wish or need, the patient may "fragment" as a manifestation of the problem

with self-cohesiveness. The symptoms of fragmentation or lack of solid self-cohesiveness can include hypochondriacal complaints and feelings of bodily disconnection or awkwardness or be behaviorally evident in the patient's aloofness and arrogance. [*Translation*: If the patient doesn't get the attention he wants, he develops symptoms of hypochondriasis, dissociation, aloofness, or arrogance.]

Having hacked our way through a jungle of jargon, lo and behold, there in the clearing is the trauma theory once again. It would say, if allowed to, "The patient had a series of traumatic events, those of being ignored instead of praised for his accomplishments. There were painful feelings that arose from being ignored, and to protect himself from experiencing those feelings again in the face of inadequate attention, the patient develops symptoms of hypochondriasis, aloofness, arrogance, etc.

English, it is true, is an imperfect language. Therefore, we should treat it gently and permit it to fulfill its function of communication as best it can. Subjecting it to such violent verbal abuse interferes with that function.

These authorities, however, treat it in the style of the unknown author of a bumper sticker that I recently saw. Unfortunately, they lack his humor and his brevity. Nonetheless, they should follow his advice, "Eschew Obsfucation."

The verbal abuse described above does serve a purpose, though, since some readers equate complexity with profundity and will respond to the author's exhibitionistic displays. That purpose, however, is merely a self-aggrandizing one, and I can well anticipate being treated with aloofness or arrogance because I did not have the proper gleam in my eye when quoting those unnecessarily ponderous passages.

There is another problem with such complex theorizing. The more complicated the theory, the more complicated the therapy becomes and the longer it lasts. This is of no demonstrable benefit to the patient, although it may be of help to the therapist, since it offers him the happy illusion that he's accomplishing more.

Baker and Baker (1987, p. 1), also writing about Kohut, say:

> While Kohut has no doubt that conflicts, particularly oedipal con-
> flicts, exist, he holds that they would be resolved without neurotic
> defenses were it not for the failure of parents to meet certain essential
> needs of the child. Kohut has gone so far as to state: "We could say
> that after an eighty-year-long detour, we are returning to Freud's
> original seduction theory—though not in the form in which Freud
> had entertained it. The seduction that we have in mind related not to
> overt sexual activities of the adult . . . but to the fact that [parents'
> empathic responsiveness to their children] is distorted in specific ways."

Here we have a statement in comprehensible English: Kohut has
recognized that basically he is using Freud's seduction theory but
without a seduction. The seduction theory without a seduction is
really nothing more than the trauma theory.

A brief aside: it's interesting to note that two renowned psychoanalysts, Kernberg and Kohut, each treating the same diagnostic category, find different dynamics in the origin of the problem, and each has
patients to confirm his theory. To me, this is one more example of
why we cannot use data from the patient to confirm whatever theory
we may be using.

Now, having looked at the work of some psychoanalysts, let's look
at the work of an analytically oriented psychotherapist, Robert
Langs. Langs (1973, p. 262) says:

> In essence, these symptoms (and neurotic disturbances) are prompt-
> ed by traumatic reality situations which create intrapsychic conflicts
> that tax the ego beyond its adaptive capacities. Experiences such as the
> birth of a sibling, the loss of a parent or sibling, a surgical procedure,
> an accident, or a seduction evoke direct fears, intrapsychic anxieties,
> and conscious and unconscious fantasies. . . . The latter are laden with
> instinctual drive wishes of sexual and aggressive nature. These wishes
> evoke anxiety because they are seen as dangers (as "forbidden") that
> will lead to personal harm (bodily damage, loss of love, condemna-

tion, etc.). This anxiety prompts the ego into action, primarily through intrapsychic defenses, in an effort to ward off these dangerous id wishes and to repress them. If these defenses are successful, a constructive synthesis of all the claims placed on the person (his ego) will result. This constitutes an adaptive response and no symptoms will appear.

On the other hand, if the ego's defensive and synthetic capacities are overtaxed, a compromise which includes mental representation from the external reality, id, superego, and ego (primarily defenses) will be made. This compromise is the symptom.

Again, the trauma theory, ornamented with psychiatric terminology and a two-stage trauma: first, a "traumatic reality situation" which disables the patient so he cannot prevent the second trauma, the emergence of fantasies, conscious and unconscious, which scare him even more painfully. His symptom, the "compromise," is to ward off this resultant anxiety.

Let us look next at an analytically oriented therapist who advocates brief therapy, James Mann (1981, p. 33):

> In the historical data, we look for recurrent events which have been provocative of pain in the life of the patient. . . . Therefore, we extract out of the historical data what we understand to be the patient's present and chronically endured pain. . . . It is a statement that is preconscious; that is to say, it is a chronic feeling about the self that periodically flits into consciousness but is equally quickly suppressed, denied, and warded off from full awareness by bringing into use well established coping devices.

Here, too, we see the trauma theory: Mann's "recurrent events" are the traumatic events that have been provocative of pain. The "well established coping devices" are the symptoms that protect the patient from experiencing (or "ward off") those feelings again.

Gustafson (1986) is an interesting brief therapist who dwells only partially in the analytic field. One of the most interesting aspects of his work is how he simultaneously draws upon the theories and therapies of other fields. He proposes that therapeutic work is best done if the therapist keeps four perspectives in mind: (1) the intrapsychic, which he calls the "analytic," (2) the analysis of "character," which is manifest by a constant attitude on the part of the patient, (3) the interpersonal perspective, which gives a view of the security operations a patient uses to make himself "worthwhile in relation to other people," and (4) the "systems perspective," in which it can be seen that the symptoms are basically protecting the whole family system.

One of the cases that Gustafson uses to illustrate the systemic perspective is "A Case of Bulimia" (pp. 230–235). This is a well presented case, handled with sensitivity and skill. My brief version of it contains none of the richness of the original.

The patient was a young woman who was scheduled to graduate with a master's degree in four months. Over the Christmas holidays she had confessed to her family that she had been bulimic for six years. In the first interview, Gustafson learned that this symptom was much worse when she was at home.

She had been vigorous and successful until junior high, when she "lost confidence" in her athletic abilities. The bulimia started when she left home to go to college, and in college her academic achievements diminished in stages, so that now her graduation was in jeopardy. Additionally, she verbally degraded herself in many ways.

Gustafson's first major intervention was the message that she *could* do well, be well, and be self-confident, but they needed to understand why she had to "distract" herself from her capabilities.

As therapy proceeds, we learn that if the patient were successful and if she did as she pleased, this would be seen as a threat to her mother, who had a need to be important by making sacrifices on behalf of her ten children. These sacrifices could only be important if her children were unsuccessful and thus dependent on their mother. Later, "success" was seen to include sexual success, the excitement of which would disrupt the "even keel" that her mother valued so highly.

As therapy proceeded further, the patient improved dramatically. (One should read the case to appreciate the maneuvers Gustafson employed to facilitate that improvement.) She spoke with pride of her accomplishments, but then became embarrassed and said that it was wrong to be boastful. This led to the discovery that her mother had been dead set against her becoming really good at something.

Gustafson responded that if she really got good at something, her mother would be less useful and less powerful. This had a telling effect, and at her next, and last, session, the patient reported that she was now doing very well in school and was quite pleased with herself in general.

There were many other aspects of the case, including how the patient's illness not only helped her mother, as mentioned above, but how it allowed her mother to "keep distance" between the patient and her father. The illness, in summary, was used to stabilize the family.

Gustafson doesn't explain what compelled this patient to protect her family when there were nine other children who could have done so, nor does he explain why, if the bingeing aspect of the bulimia was a symptom which served to protect the family, she kept it a secret for six years. Without these explanations, I cannot be sure that his fourth perspective, the systemic one, is in accord with the trauma theory, but let's look at the other three perspectives. To do so, I'm forced to use a hypothetical approach.

Had someone with my perspective seen this case, which did not happen, and had the techniques like I use worked, which often happens, but not always, it's likely that something of this nature would have occurred:

All of the initial symptoms would have been "lumped" as self-defeating behavior. Probably we would have found a series of traumatic events in which the mother had hurt the patient for being "really good at something," and the patient began protecting *herself*, not mother, by becoming less good at virtually everything, and even bad mouthed herself so any achievements could be hidden.

This is what I hypothesize would have been found from Gustafson's first perspective, the analytic one. It would explain the second perspective, the "constant attitude" of being clumsy, inept, etc., and it would also explain the third perspective, making herself "worthwhile" to others. She became worthwhile to her parents by being dependent, and she was at least acceptable to others, according to her mother's standards, by not becoming too good at anything.

Finally, her symptoms might indeed have protected the family system, but in my mind, at least, it's questionable if that was the primary function of the symptoms or if it were a mere by-product of her self-protection. Part of the self-protection was mentioned above; in addition, it is clear that protecting the family from floundering is highly self-protective. The patient is a member of the family, and thus would be one of those floundering.

So, we see that various forms of analytic therapy all employ the trauma theory, dressing it in fancy frills and calling it different names. What about the nonanalytic therapies?

Before moving to those, I'll discuss briefly another form of therapy, "Redecision Therapy," developed by Goulding and Goulding (1979). Although I imagine that both Freudian and redecision therapists would be equally distressed to have this form of therapy described as "analytic," I believe that it is. It analyzes symptoms, though, rather than hypothesized infantile drives, transferences, and resistances.

To briefly sum up the analytic aspect of this therapy: Patients are "brought back," with or without hypnotic techniques, to a time in their lives when they "decided" to respond in some way that is now labeled symptomatic. It can be seen from what they describe as happening to them at that time that the decision to respond in this symptomatic way was an effort to protect themselves from painful feelings that were occurring then.

Once more, the trauma theory. Incidentally, the "corridor of time" technique that will be described a bit later in this book contains all of the essential ingredients of this form of therapy.

Next, let us look at behavior therapy. It is generally considered far removed from the traditional analytic point of view. Certainly the practice of behavior therapy is far different from the practice of psychoanalysis—but are there similarities in the basic underlying theory? If, first, we can agree that the trauma theory is the foundation for the beliefs about symptom formation according to the analysts, and second, we can get beyond the jargon of the behaviorists, then I'd like to make the point that they do not differ at all.

Behavioral therapists believed that symptoms are "learned behavior." What does this mean? It certainly doesn't mean that Little Johnny, Little Hans, or anyone else learned this behavior because one day his teacher said, "Little Johnny, come to the front of the room. I'd like to teach you a symptom."

Behaviorists believe that Johnny "learned" his symptom because he responded in what is now a symptomatic manner to some sort of traumatic experience or series of experiences. If his response had produced *more* distress, it would have become "extinguished." It's because the response provided some protection that it was "reinforced" and persisted. I fail to see that this is anything other than the trauma theory, despite such terms as "one trial learning" or "conditioned responses."

Those family or systems therapies that deal only with current issues in the life of the patient and his or her family are also working on the same basic theory. For example, when a child develops symptoms as a consequence of severe parental discord, one can easily see that this discord is a traumatic event to the child. It causes painful feelings, and the problematic behavior that he displays is his attempt to protect himself from those feelings. One could claim, as Gustafson did in his case, that the symptoms serve not to protect himself, but really to distract the parents from their unhappiness. What difference does it make? It's by protecting the parents from their problems that the child is protected from his feared loss of one or both of them.

What about rational therapy? Ellis (1977) says, " . . . disturbed human beings act in an irrational and self-defeating manner because they believe, quite falsely, that they are helping themselves thereby." My interpretation of this would be that they believe, consciously or otherwise, that their symptomatic behavior is protecting them from some danger or gaining them some reward.

He says that these ideas are ones which they previously learned from their parents and their culture. In the case that he presents to illustrate his ideas and technique, "The Treatment of a Psychopath with Rational Psychotherapy," Ellis says, "Jim's severe feelings of inadequacy—his original feelings that he never could gain the attention of others unless he was a problem child . . . were also traced to the self-propagated beliefs behind them (p. 260)." It's unlikely that Jim's parents and teachers ever told him, "You're never going to gain the attention of others unless you're a problem child." If he learned this illogical message from his parents or his culture, then presumably it was on the basis of the way that others responded to him. Those responses must have been seen as traumatic.

What about cognitive therapy? Cognitive therapists, at least in dealing with depression, believe that the basic pathology is the "cognitive triad," that is, (1) a negative view of the self, (2) an interpretation of ongoing events in a negative way, and (3) a negative view of the future. They believe that early experiences form the basis for developing this triad and that it can be precipitated by specific circumstances that are analogous to those early experiences.

Can we say that this is also an example of using the trauma theory? It's safe to assume that delightful early experiences are unlikely to cause negative views, so perhaps it's also safe to assume that the early experiences to which they refer were traumatic. It then follows that any traumatic experience would cause painful feelings. But how would this negative triad protect the patient from experiencing those painful feelings again?

At least at first, an expression of these views will often cause friends to rally round with sympathy and support and to proclaim, "Cheer up, things aren't really that bad." Or, "You just need to get out and have some fun. How about going to a movie with me tonight?"

I believe that there's much more to it than that, though. In patients whom I've seen, this negative view of the self was often designed to spur the patient to renewed effort to make himself better, thus helping to protect him from criticism or from the pain of failure. It didn't work, of course, in those people who became patients, but that was its design.

The negative view of the present, in patients whom I've seen, was often the result of earlier experiences that had taught them that bad things would always happen whenever things were going too well. Thus, by denying that things were going well, they could magically ward off another bad and painful experience. The negative view of the future was designed in much the same way, to ward off the bitter disappointments that had occurred repeatedly when promised pleasures had not materialized.

We've now looked at a number of different theoretical formulations, demonstrating that in each the trauma theory has merely been translated into new and often complex terminology. Since I personally see no merit in expressing it in terms that are less rather than more easily understood, perhaps we should stick to the early Freudian concept in its simple form.

I cannot claim that this theory is the basis for all of the 200 to 400 therapies that exist—I cannot even claim the ability to name most of them—but it does seem to be the basis for enough of them for us to proceed.

Implications of the Simple Theory

The primary implication of this theory is that a symptom is a protective device, intended to prevent the patient from reexperiencing feelings that were intolerably painful to him/her. Consequently, even if the symptom is not doing its job too well, the patient will be reluctant to give it up until either of two things happens: S/he becomes convinced that the old dangers no longer exist, or s/he learns that there are better ways of protecting oneself.

Corollary to the Trauma Theory

The patient, instead of having had a traumatic experience that caused painful feelings that s/he is trying to avoid, may have had an exceptionally pleasant experience that gave him/her exceptionally pleasant feelings. The symptom is designed to help him/her recapture those good feelings again and again.

It takes no great leap of faith for me to believe that the trauma theory and its corollary explain why patients behave as they do. I think they are the basis for our behaving as we do. Our actions are designed to protect us from danger or to provide us with pleasure, at least in the broadest sense of either concept. The dangers or pleasures may be internal or external, real or imagined, conscious or not. Therefore, the only real difference I see between normal behavior and symptomatic behavior is that one works well or is quickly altered, and the other doesn't work well and is repeated over and over.

This idea of protection and gratification can also be traced back to Freud. He told us that within our inner world there lies an id, propelling us toward those pleasures that come from being bad. There is also a superego, propelling us toward those pleasures that come from being good and simultaneously protecting us by its warnings not to heed the evil urgings of the id. Additionally, there is an ego, which helps us avoid the dangers of the outer world and obtain some of the gratifications that are available there. It also mediates between the id and the superego, and even constructs mechanisms of defense to protect us from the superego making us feel bad when the id tries to make us feel good.

The original description was a bit more technical.

3 | THERAPEUTIC IMPLICATIONS OF THE TRAUMA THEORY

IF ONE WERE TO USE the trauma theory—not necessarily because it's true, but because a theory helps give direction to therapy—then one might engage in a straightforward, uncomplicated therapy that consists of four basic steps. These provide insight into the origin of the symptoms and rapid relief of them.

1. Uncover the original trauma(s).
2. Learn the painful feelings that the trauma(s) caused.
3. Understand how the symptom protects the patient from having those feelings again.
4. Help the patient understand either that the old dangers no longer exist or that there are better ways of protecting oneself.

These last two steps differ slightly from what I had written before (Edelstein, 1981, p. 129). Then I believed that attenuating the feelings was the third step; now I believe that understanding their protective function is more valuable. Then I listed as step four, "helping the patient learn how to face new situations unencumbered by the effects of his prior experiences." My current fourth step, I believe, says the same thing, but is more specific as to how to do this.

The first three steps provide "insight," and the last provides "therapy." A number of different theoretical schools have demonstrated that step number four is all that's really essential for symptoms to be reduced or eliminated entirely, and I'll discuss that in much greater detail. But first I'll try to deal with the question, "If the fourth step is all that's essential, why bother with the first three?"

It's true that the first three steps are not necessary, or not always necessary, but there are certain values that I attach to them anyway. From my own perspective, I always feel more comfortable if I know (or believe I know) what caused the symptom before I try to remove it. This is an honored and often important medical tradition. From the patients' perspective, many of them want to know "why?" When we can quickly find an answer that seems to satisfy that question, they deserve to know.

The most important reason, however, is this: In the fourth step patients are to realize that the old dangers no longer exist, and they can come to that realization more easily when they know what the old dangers were. They are to believe that there are better ways of protecting themselves, and they can more readily accept those new ways if they understand the dangers from which they needed protection. In other words, the first three steps can speed up the therapeutic process *if* they can be accomplished quickly, and now there are a variety of techniques available to do that. I'll describe some of them a little later.

A number of modern therapies rely primarily on the fourth step, believing that "insight" is of little or no value. Even though I disagree, I readily concede that the information obtained to explain the "why" is always of such dubious validity that they may be right. For example, does the explanation lie in a prior life? A birth trauma? Infantile drives? Early childhood or adolescent experiences? Current problems? Family interactions? Even the last two, which should contain the least distortion due to the passage of time, may be revealed to us in badly distorted forms, as anyone who has ever done couples or family therapy knows. More ancient problems, presumably, are subject to even greater distortion.

Before going into an explanation of how I, and others, employ the four steps for insight-oriented therapy, let's look briefly at some of those therapies that rely on the fourth step alone.

I believe that behavior therapy, at least in some of its more popular aspects, utilizes this step beautifully. With either progressive desensitization, in which the patient is gradually exposed to increasingly proximal confrontations with his feared object or situation and then relaxed between each confrontation, or flooding, a technique in which the patient is abruptly exposed to the full intensity of his feared object or situation and forced to cringe in fear until the fear has passed, we can see: "Look, you faced this object or situation and no harm came to you. The danger you feared no longer exists."

"Adverse conditioning" is anther behavioral technique. In this, patients are given some objectionable treatment when they display the symptom that is to be cured. For example, alcoholics may be given medication that makes them vomit each time they take a drink. Those with other conditions could be given an electrical shock or some other unpleasant stimulus each time they act in the symptomatic way. The treatment itself becomes a traumatic event causing painful feelings, and to protect themselves from having those painful feelings again, patients adopt (in theory) a new set of behaviors, i.e., not drinking or not displaying old symptoms. Since this new behavior is considered "constructive," it is not called a symptom. Unfortunately or fortunately, depending upon one's perspective, patients may protect themselves by a different set of new behaviors—dropping out of treatment. Since this would not be considered constructive, it could be called a new symptom, and that symptom could be given a specific name, "resistance," although this is not a term that behaviorists use very often.

When the behavior therapist uses "positive reinforcement," that is, when he gives the patient a reward for displaying new and better behavior, we see a perfect example of the corollary of the trauma theory.

In strategic therapy, the therapist offers the patient new ways of dealing with whatever problem the patient presents. That is exactly in accord with step four, learning better ways to protect oneself. For example, if a mother reports, "My son leaves his clothes and books all over the house and no matter how much I yell and scream at him, he never remembers to pick them up," the therapist might suggest, "Instead of yelling at him for not picking them up, why not just throw them in the garbage? His behavior will probably change."

This little scenario is an example both of the trauma theory and of step four. For the mother, the books being left all over the house is a traumatic event causing painful feelings because she interprets the mess as meaning that she's not loved, not appreciated, powerless, etc. The yelling is designed to protect her from experiencing those bad feelings again. The strategic therapist employs step four and offers her a better(?) way to protect herself; s/he probably will not attempt to do insight-oriented work to help her understand what earlier experiences might have sensitized her and led to her current responses.

In cognitive therapy the task of the therapist is to expunge the patient of the "negative triad": the negative view of oneself, the world in which one lives, and the future. The therapist employs a series of techniques to do this. S/he points out and dissuades the patient from using old coping mechanisms like: (1) arbitrary inferences, in which conclusions are formed without adequate evidence; (2) selective abstractions, which involve focus on details out of context; (3) overgeneralization, which means reaching general conclusions based on isolated incidents; (4) magnification and minimization, that is, the distortion of the significance of events; (5) personalization, which is relating things to oneself without basis; and (6) absolute dichotomous thinking, or seeing everything as black or white.

Please note: When patients engage in the six errors mentioned above, they might develop depression. When therapists engage in the six errors mentioned above they might develop a new psychiatric theory. There are examples of at least the first four errors in this book, and anyone who looks closely will probably find them in virtually any other book on psychiatric theory.

If the cognitive therapist succeeds in this task, what has been accomplished? S/he has gradually allowed the patient to see that old methods of protection are no longer needed and to realize that the old dangers no longer exist. I believe those dangers are the ones I discussed in Chapter 2. (1) The fear of criticism from others, or the fear of failure leads to seeing oneself negatively as an (ineffective) incentive to become better. (2) The fear of good things changing to bad leads to a negative view of the present, with an almost magical expectation that seeing things badly will prevent their becoming bad. (3) The fear of future disappointments leads to a negative view of the future, so, if it's viewed negatively already, there will be no reason to be disappointed.

In rational therapy a concerted attack is made on patients' irrational beliefs, and they are urged or commanded into "emotionally reeducating activity." The irrational beliefs attacked in this way are either beliefs that a danger exists when in fact that is no longer true or beliefs that one has a satisfactory method of protecting oneself when the method is actually the symptomatic behavior. The "emotionally reeducating activity" turns out to be either a demonstration that one can act in a nonsymptomatic way without incurring harm or a new and better way of protecting oneself from the old dangers.

In solution-oriented therapy (de Shazer 1985, 1988, O'Hanlon and Weiner-Davis, 1989), the therapist, instead of offering the patient new ways to deal with problems, helps the patient find those occasions in which the patient dealt with them well in the past. S/he then has the patient do more of the same thing. I believe that these "solutions" are essentially better ways of protecting oneself.

If neither the patient nor the therapist can find even a single time in which the patient handled a similar situation well, the therapist will "prescribe" some change in the pattern of dealing with the problem. The change may be simple, for instance, merely altering the time, place, or circumstances in which the problem occurs. Or the alterations may be complicated, funny, or even bizarre. One example offered by a student of O'Hanlon's involved a couple who frequently engaged in foolish arguments. He prescribed that anytime they started arguing they should go into the bathroom. The husband was then to lie down in the tub and his wife was to sit upon the closed toilet lid as they continued their argument. They tried but couldn't continue the arguments because they would start laughing at the absurdity of their situation. After a while, when an argument seemed to be building up, one of them would merely look in the direction of the bathroom, they'd both start laughing, and the argument would lose its momentum.

Here is an example of one of the very few times that I have tried doing something similar. The patient was seen in our crisis group, complaining of excess, unbearable, self-generated stress on her job. She was responsible for writing reports for her company, and even though her second draft always won the admiration of her co-workers, she felt compelled to take her work home and write a third, fourth, sixth, or even eighth draft. Consequently she was up late every night, was worn out every day, had almost no time for her husband, and found no joy in life.

I asked if she would follow some advice that I wished to give, and she impulsively agreed to do so, without first hearing what it would be. I told her that if she wanted to write perfectly, it would only be appropriate for her to look perfect when she did so. Therefore, if ever she went beyond a second draft, she was to bathe, do her hair and makeup, dress in her finest party dress, and put on her best jewelry before returning to the typewriter. She looked at me rather strangely, as did my co-therapist, but said, "Okay."

She returned the next week and gave us her report. She had been in her office, had just finished the second draft of a report, and was planning to begin her third. Since she was in the office, she couldn't follow my advice, so she decided to walk around the block instead.

During her walk she decided that she was only being paid to work 40 hours a week, so it was foolish to work 80. She returned to the office, showed her second draft to her boss, who liked it except for one small change in the second paragraph. She made the suggested change and turned it in. When she started to leave for home that afternoon, she began loading her briefcase with work to do that evening, remembered my advice, and left the briefcase at the office. Since then, she and her husband had been enjoying life together again.

I suspect that the absurdity of my advice helped her recognize the absurdity of her protective actions, and whatever "dangers" she had been avoiding paled in comparison.

Although this change was dramatic, it was also transient. After her second session in the crisis group, she was referred to our cognitive therapy group, and one of the co-leaders of that group later told me that the obsessive behavior had returned. It seemed to respond quite well to cognitive therapy, however, and some months after finishing that group the patient wrote the therapist a letter saying how well she was doing.

My amateurish excursion into solution-oriented therapy should not be taken as a criticism of that style of therapy, for it seems to work well for those who are versed in it. Moreover, the two examples that I offered should not be viewed as indicating that it consists entirely of absurd prescriptions. There is obviously much more to it than that.

Milton Erickson originated many of the ideas that have been developed into strategic and solution-oriented therapies. He was known primarily as a hypnotherapist, but much of the work he did did not utilize hypnosis—or at least not in any way that one would ordinarily define it (there is no good definition of hypnosis, but that doesn't stop people from ordinarily defining it).

Despite all that has been written about him, it is impossible for me to know what system of therapy Erickson used, other than the system of doing "whatever works," which, when one thinks about it, is probably better than most of the other systems that any of us employs.

One of his one-visit cures (Haley, 1985) involved his making a house call to the home of a 14-year-old girl who would not leave her home because she was so ashamed of her feet, which she perceived to be "too large." He carried on a conversation with her parents for a while, arose, stepped backwards, and "accidentally" stomped on the patient's toes. He yelled at her, "If you would grow those things *large* enough for a *man* to see, I wouldn't be in this situation" (p. 14). That cured her. I view this as a perfect, if somewhat radical, example of helping the patient recognize that the danger she feared was no longer present.

I must add that, although I admire the way this worked for Erickson, if I tried the same thing I'd probably end up with a patient who wouldn't leave the house because she feared people would always be stepping on her small feet.

Having looked at a number of different therapies from this perspective, I begin to wonder how different one is from another, except for the rituals involved. Beitman, Goldfried, and Norcross (1989) state, "There is a growing tendency among psychotherapists to ignore the ideological barriers dividing schools of psychotherapy and to define what is common among them and what is useful in each of them."

One thing that is common among the insight-oriented therapies is that they all attempt to help patients find a trauma that will explain why they act, feel, or think the way they do. The trauma sought will vary considerably depending upon the therapist's orientation. Thus, we have trauma related to infantile drives or fantasies vs. trauma that occurred later in life. There are also traumas that occurred earlier than the infantile fantasies, if we wish to include those therapies that believe in the birth trauma or in past lives.

Uncovering the emotions generated by those trauma seems to be something else shared by the insight-oriented therapies. They then have a great variety of methods for dealing with those emotions.

To define what is common among *all* the therapies, insight-oriented or not, a case could be made that they all accomplish step four, i.e., they help the patient understand that there is no current danger or that there are better ways of protecting oneself from those dangers that might exist.

In defining what is *useful* among all the therapies, my vote would go to those things that help the patient *respond* in a new and better way. The new and better responses might be in thinking, feeling, behavior, or physiology.

To obtain new and better thinking, the therapist may do something as simple as reframe a situation for the patient. For example: "I certainly understand that it bothers you for the children to always fight over who gets to ride in the front seat, but you must be flattered to know that they both love you enough to want to be next to you." The therapist may help improve the patient's thinking by using rational therapy or cognitive therapy.

To obtain better feeling responses, the therapist could use the above techniques, for once a change occurs in the way the patient thinks about something, the feelings about it will also change. Or the therapist could use a more direct approach, say with behavior therapy: "Now that you've stayed in this supermarket until your fear subsided, you won't be as frightened of supermarkets anymore."

To obtain new behavior, the therapist could use any of the above techniques, for once patients think or feel differently about something, they have the freedom to behave differently. Or he could use a more direct approach, as with solution-oriented therapy, "Next time the two of you begin an argument, go into the bathroom. You lie down in the tub and you sit on the toilet seat. Then continue the argument, if you can." Or he could use strategic therapy, "Instead of yelling when he leaves his clothes on the floor, just let them stay there until they rot."

To obtain any of the above, at least in certain diagnostic categories, the therapist may prescribe medication, and improvement will occur in each of the areas.

This general principle was illustrated nicely by Munoz (1988). He reported on a study in which depressed patients were divided into groups and each group received 12 weeks of therapy. One group was treated by having patients engage in more activities of any sort that made them feel better. A second group was given cognitive therapy, and a third group, interpersonal therapy. All three groups improved to essentially the same degree. The activity group developed less negative thinking, more positive thinking, and displayed better inter-personal activity. The cognitive therapy group became more active and engaged in more socializing. The interpersonal group became more active and had less negative thinking and more positive think-ing. We have all seen that a depressed patient, once responding well to antidepressant medication, displays improvement in all these areas.

These are my reasons for believing that what is useful in any therapy is helping the patient to respond in a new and better way. It is interesting to wonder if long-term therapy takes so long primarily because the therapist generally spends such a small percentage of his time in these activities and so much of his time in merely letting the patient "understand" things about himself.

Gaining understanding about oneself is different from gaining un-derstanding about a symptom per se, for the latter can be quite effective in promoting new responses. Gustafson (1986), who is cer-tainly a believer in brief psychotherapy, maintains that understanding why one has stayed the same is basically what is needed to enable change. From my perspective, this means that the patient is helped to understand why the symptom had been viewed as a protective device and to realize that it is no longer needed.

In looking at what is useful in the therapies, we must realize that nothing is useful unless the particular therapist can use it with the particular patient. Some patients who might respond beautifully to one technique may not respond to another. Not all therapists are able to use all techniques.

I, for example, would probably do very poorly with those tech-niques that involve constant, forceful confrontations with patients, for that does not fit my personality. Nor would I do well with past lives regression therapy, for that does not fit well with my sense of the sensible.

I've taught many professionals how to use the hypnotic techniques described in this book. Some of them take to hypnosis like ducks take to water; others like ducks to hot concrete.

It's well to try to decide what is useful in the different therapies and important to realize that whatever is useful can probably be accomplished in a number of ways. As therapists, we owe it to our patients to know at least several of those ways, for it seems as inappropriate for the psychotherapist to know only one method of therapy as it would be for the pharmacotherapist to know only one medication.

.

4 | CONSIDERATIONS REGARDING THE VALUE OF BRIEF THERAPIES

FOR THE MOST PART, the analytically oriented therapists believe as Langs does (1973, p. 264): "Unconscious fantasies are the key to the neuroses, and their derivatives must be detected and analyzed if genuine symptom relief through intrapsychic change is to occur." This bold, unequivocal claim, if true, would indicate that all other forms of therapy are of no genuine value. However, there is no evidence that this claim is true, except for the teachings of other analytically oriented therapists, none of whom is able to offer proof.

Meanwhile, many therapists apparently are doing very successful therapy without detecting and analyzing the derivatives of these unconscious fantasies. This makes the validity of Langs' claim highly questionable. We must wonder, then, if this claim, despite its boldness, is nothing more than a rationalization for the continuance of long-term, analytically oriented treatment.

Frank (1965, p. 92), for example, states:

> The regression to these pre-traumatic fixation points may offer excellent research opportunities for the study of personality development. But therapeutically they are not relevant. Often we find that the patient regresses in his free associations to conflictual early infantile material as a maneuver to evade the essential pathogenic conflicts

which occurred later. This material appears as "deep material" and both patient and therapist in mutual self deception spend a great deal of time and effort in analyzing this essentially evasive material.

In other words, while the analytically oriented therapist sees traumatic events that occurred later in life as screens to ward off the remembrance of earlier infantile conflicts, therapists like Frank believe the infantile issues are screens to ward off remembrance of the traumatic events of some later periods. There is no evidence that either belief produces benefits that are longer lasting, but there is a mountain of evidence that the analytic approach produces therapy that is longer lasting, often by a number of years.

If Crews is correct about Freud's lack of therapeutic success, then there is the distinct possibility that his failures were the direct result of analyzing "this essentially evasive material," the infantile conflicts, rather than attending to "the essential pathogenic conflicts which occurred later."

Still, Langs' claim should not be taken lightly. The analysts believe that the short-term therapies are superficial and that there is a high degree of probability that symptoms, if removed at all, will return or will be replaced by other symptoms. This, of course, implies that profound and permanent changes occur with psychoanalysis.

What is the evidence to prove or disprove the damning predictions about short-term therapy? Luborsky, Singer, and Luborsky (1975), not specifically attending to the duration of symptom removal, reviewed a number of different studies by a variety of researchers who had looked at the outcomes of the various psychotherapies. Among the conclusions from all of those different studies were (1) "most comparative studies of different forms of psychotherapy found insignificant differences in proportions of patients who improved by the end of psychotherapy," and (2) brief therapies do not seem inferior to long-term therapy. In another overview, Andrews and Harvey (1981), reviewing 475 controlled studies in which the median duration of therapy was only 15 hours, found that the typical patient after therapy was better off than 77% of untreated controls.

These reviews seem to contradict Langs' contention about the quality of therapies. What about the duration of the benefits? Nicholson and Berman (1983) reviewed follow-up research to see how outcomes when treatment ended compared to outcomes at follow-up. The studies that they reviewed included: (a) a direct search of the volumes of journals publishing psychotherapy research from 1960 to 1979; (b) previous reviews of the outcome literature; (c) the bibliographies of located studies; and (d) *Psychological Abstracts*, 1960 to 1980. After this extensive review they state:

> Results of the review demonstrated that information obtained at follow-up often added little to that obtained at the end of treatment. *The findings highlight the general durability of gains achieved during psychotherapy*, suggesting that costly follow-up procedures may be used more selectively. (emphasis mine) (pp. 261–278)

The Luborskys' report, however, did not include studies of psychoanalysis. Lewin (1970, p. 250) writes, "In 1967 the American Psychoanalytic Association released their finding of long-term sociologic and statistical study of the results of treatment by psychoanalysis and analytic psychotherapy. While 97% of the patients were judged by their therapists to have improved in total functioning, and a similar number of patients agreed, the over all rate of symptom cure was only 27%." In other words, analysts could claim that in 73% of their cases there was no *return* of symptoms—simply because the symptoms never went away in the first place. Just how important would that claim be?

Malcolm (1981, p. 107) quotes "Dr. Aaron" on the results of psychoanalysis. (Dr. Aaron is a member of the New York Psychoanalytic Institute, or at least he was when Malcolm wrote the book; if the members of the institute paid attention to what he said, they may have run him out of town on a rail by now.)

> And the changes achieved are very small. We live our lives according to the repetition compulsion, and analysis can go only so far in freeing

us from it. Analysis leaves the patient with more freedom of choice than he had before—but how much more? This much: instead of going straight down the meridian, he will go 5%, 10%—maybe 15% if you push very hard—to the left or to the right, but no more than that.

Does this 5–10% improvement represent the profound benefit of psychoanalysis? When I get that kind of result I consider it a therapeutic failure, and the patient should as well. It's a little scary to believe that other therapists view this as a desirable goal.

Aaron's comments about the efficacy of psychoanalysis should be thoroughly disturbing to any analytically oriented therapist, except, perhaps, for the fact that they were preconditioned by Freud, who said (1937), "One ought not to be surprised if it should turn out . . . that the difference between a person who has been analyzed and the behavior of a person after he has been analysed is not so thoroughgoing as we aim at making it and as we expect and maintain it to be." Maybe the analytically oriented therapists were not preconditioned; maybe they just weren't paying attention.

Aaron is also quoted by Malcolm (p. 59):

> Our institute is large, and the places in the inner sanctum are limited. Many of those who don't make it—become bitter. They are the reason for the discontent, antagonism, backbiting, and factionalism of our institute, for the constant danger of schism. As for the ones who do make it, their behavior is like that of uneasy, shifty-eyed "good children" who have got into favor with their parents at the expense of their siblings—they are keeping the other children out, and they feel guilty and defensive because they're afraid they didn't get in there fairly.

To me, this sounds like as unpleasant and as maladapted a group of people as any I'd ever wish to meet. It's true that similar descriptions might be made of in and out groups in other large organizations, but there's a difference that cannot be overlooked: We *know* that the people Aaron is describing have been through at least one analysis, because that's a rule of the analytic institute, and we also know that they've been analyzed by "training analysts" (the "shifty-eyed good children"), who are regarded as among the best. So what does this say about the benefits of psychoanalysis? There are at least three possibilities:

1. The members of the institute were reasonably normal when they entered analysis and became this disturbed after being analyzed.
2. They were this disturbed to begin with, and the analysis brought about little change.
3. The institute's careful selection process chooses exceptionally maladjusted candidates, who, after significant benefit from analysis are only this badly maladjusted.

There is, of course, a fourth possibility. Aaron's observations may be totally inaccurate. It may be that he sees his colleagues in a highly distorted and unflattering light. If so, that indicates that either (a) his extensive training in the institute failed to give him the objectivity and perception that one would expect in an even minimally qualified therapist, thus raising doubt about the quality of training, or (b) his training was excellent, but his own severe neurotic tendencies create this unwarranted distortion. If the latter is true, then the first three possibilities are applicable to Aaron, if not to his colleagues.

On the issue of symptom substitution, let me refer to Aaron one final time. On page 59 he tells Malcolm that after his *second* analysis he developed substitute symptoms: anxiety about crowds, being in a theater, and public speaking. These symptoms were interfering with his professional advancement, and he was considering a *third* analysis to cure him of the symptoms that resulted from his second one.

Now Dr. Aaron represents only one case, and we shouldn't generalize too broadly from his experience. Still, he is an analyst and a dedicated proponent of psychoanalysis, and yet he gives these devas-

tating descriptions of his institute, the value of psychoanalysis generally, and his own in particular. After two analyses, he still needs a third,
and this is in line with Lewin's report that, although 97% of patients
felt the analysis had been useful, only a fourth of them experienced
cure of their symptoms. It also points out that if the short-term
therapies produce substitute symptoms, they're not the only ones that
do so.

So, until the advocates of long-term analytically oriented therapies
have better evidence that theirs is the superior form of treatment, it
seems reasonable to go along with those therapies that more quickly
accomplish, by whatever means, step four. That step, learning that
the old dangers no longer exist or that there are better ways of
protecting oneself from those dangers, is not unlike Alexander and
French's (1974) "corrective emotional experience," which in turn is
similar to Kohut's belief, as explained by Cooper (1983, p. 5),
"Whereas traditional analysis has advanced interpretation as the psy-
choanalyst's basic therapeutic action, Kohut emphasizes the analyst's
creation of a *new kind of experience* for the patient within the transference relationship, of which interpretation is only a facet."

To say that this "corrective emotional experience" must occur "within the transference relationship" raises an interesting issue. Do we ever
have relationships in which some sort of transference is not occurring?
Probably not, and if that's true, then to say that this must occur
within a transference relationship is meaningless. If Kohut, however,
defines the transference relationship only in terms of the transference
that occurs in formal therapy, then his statement is inaccurate. I — and
many of my patients — have had profoundly beneficial "new kinds of
experiences" that occurred completely outside of any formal therapy.

So, reviewing the evidence regarding the value of short-term therapies (and there is certainly much more available than I have quoted),
we see that, generally speaking, there is no reason to believe that long-
term therapies are superior. When we get away from "generally speaking" and look at certain specific disorders, we find evidence that brief
therapies have the edge.

Some compulsions, phobias, and sexual problems respond better to behavior therapy than to analytically oriented therapies (Garfield and Bergin, 1978). Marital problems respond better to marital therapy (Gurman and Kniskern, 1978). Depression responds better to cognitive therapy.

An interesting possibility as to why psychoanalysis produces only a "5-10% difference" is that it places too much emphasis on the analysis of the patient and too little on step number four. In other words, it tries to explain why patients are the way they are without helping them fully understand that they no longer need to be that way (because the old dangers no longer exist) or without helping them in a more active fashion to find new ways of being (new ways to protect themselves from the old dangers).

Brief therapists actively encourage the patient to do things differently. Whether they use techniques to help patients understand the origin of their problems or consider the origins irrelevant, they still encourage patients to start doing things differently. They will often suggest, prescribe, order, or beg patients to try new behaviors. When patients do try these new things and see that they work well with no harm being done to anyone, they truly experience a corrective emotional experience.

II | *PSYCHOLOGICAL DISORDERS WITH OBSCURE ORIGINS*

5 | THERAPEUTIC APPLICATIONS OF THE TRAUMA THEORY

RECALLING WHAT WAS said before, the analysis of a symptom requires three steps: (1) discovering the original traumatic incident, (2) understanding what feelings were caused by that incident, and (3) seeing how the symptom protected the patient from experiencing that feeling again. In psychological disorders with obscure origins, "uncovering" or "insight" is necessary to accomplish these steps. In psychological disorders with obvious origins, no uncovering is needed, for the information is readily apparent to any interested observer. "Cure" of the symptom is then achieved by helping the patient understand that either the old dangers no longer exist or that there are better ways of protecting oneself; this is step four in the therapy that is made feasible by using the trauma theory.

Undoubtedly there are many ways of accomplishing the first three steps, just as noninsight-oriented therapies have a variety of ways of accomplishing step number four. I prefer to use hypnotic techniques for all four steps in an insight-oriented therapy, not because I believe them to be necessary, but because they work faster for me than any other techniques.

In Chapter 6 the reader will have the opportunity to see how approximately similar cases can be handled with or without hypnosis. There will be illustrative cases from a variety of authors interspersed with cases of my own. To understand a little better what I'm doing when I use hypnosis, you may wish to read about the techniques that I use. But because this is not a book about hypnosis, I will give only brief descriptions of the techniques that I use. I've described them before in much greater detail (Edelstien, 1981). Many others are available, and other therapists may have decided preferences for them.

Techniques for Steps One, Two, and Three

The techniques that I use for the first three steps are: simple age regression (essentially the same technique that Freud used when he worked with hypnosis), ideomotor signaling (Cheek and LeCron, 1968), the affect bridge (Watkins, 1971), ego state therapy (Watkins and Watkins, 1979), and the corridor of time (Author unknown).

Simple Age Regression

The hypnotized patient is told, "When I count back from three to zero, you will be able to go back to some period in your life when something happened that caused this symptom to develop. Three . . . two . . . one . . . zero. When you are back to that time in your life, nod your head so I will know. (Nod) Tell me what is happening?"

There are many variations on this simple technique that involve the patient's visualizing some situation that might transport him, or at least his thoughts and feelings, to some prior period. Twenty-five years ago the images were of being on a flying carpet, being on a train moving backwards, or flipping through the pages of a photo album, looking at earlier and earlier periods in his life.

Today, thanks to modern technology, the images might involve being in a time machine, flying in a space shuttle faster than light so that the further one travels the further one journeys into the past, or viewing a videotape played in reverse. It is not at all certain that the modern technology is superior to the old, or that any of the visualizations are superior to unadorned age regression.

Ideomotor Signaling

This technique is based upon (1) the observation that all of us display feelings by movement of facial and bodily muscles, a phenomenon commonly called "body language," and (2) the discovery that when proper suggestions are given to the hypnotized subject, s/he will move specific muscles in response to "subconscious" memories and feelings. These specific movements then form a primitive vocabulary consisting of at least "yes" and "no," enabling the therapist to understand more clearly what those subconscious memories and feelings are.

The hypnotized patient is instructed that one finger will automatically move up and down to signal "yes," a second, "no," and in a more elaborate structure, a third, "I don't know," and a fourth, "I don't want to answer that."

Although the original method of using these signals was rather long and complex, Cheek has since simplified it so that now a typical series of questions might go like this:

"Is this (symptom) the result of something that occurred before the age of twenty?" (yes)

"Before the age of ten?" (yes)

"Before the age of five?" (no)

"At six?" (no)

"Seven?" (yes)

"Good. Now I'd like your memory to orient itself to when you were seven and something happened that caused this symptom to develop. When it has done so, the "yes" finger will signal me." (yes)

"Is it all right to tell me about it?"

Along the way toward simplifying this technique, Cheek used an intermediate step after he had learned at what age the traumatic incident occurred. He first asked for the "subconscious memory" to orient itself to that period, and then he asked for the memory to come up into consciousness. He no longer uses that step. Cheek notes that *it is not necessary to hypnotize the patient before starting this.* The involuntary finger signals can occur without any formal hypnotic induction, but the patient usually seems to enter a hypnotic state during the questioning process. Rossi and Cheek (1988) give many excellent examples of how this technique can be used today.

Ego State Therapy

This technique is based on the writings of an analyst, Paul Federn, but can be more easily understood starting with the everyday observation that people frequently display very different aspects of themselves. This display may take a variety of forms: "Part of me wants to do this, but another part just won't let me," or "I know I shouldn't act that way, but something makes me do it anyhow." Or individuals may behave very differently under different circumstances: "John is usually so quiet and dignified, but when he gets together with his old college buddies he becomes loud and obnoxious. It's like he's a different person."

The "part that won't let me," the "something that makes me," and the "different person" would all be examples of ego states. It is probable that these ego states are merely metaphors, and other metaphors could be used. As a matter of fact, other metaphors are used; some therapists use "id, ego, and superego," some use "parent, child, and adult," and some even use "earth bound spirits" and believe that psychotherapy consists of "depossessing" the patient of those spirits. It's my belief that using the metaphors too concretely is a mistake.

With ego state therapy, once the patient has entered deeply enough into a hypnotic state, the therapist can speak directly to the ego state that is causing the symptom and can learn from it what was happening to the patient when the ego state was first formed. What was happening is the traumatic incident that caused the development of the symptom, and it becomes readily apparent how the symptom serves to protect the patient from experiencing again the painful feelings that were involved.

The Affect Bridge

This technique is used primarily for understanding the origin of a troubling feeling; a phobia is a good example. The hypnotized patient is told to experience that feeling now and to let it grow stronger (with care that it does not become too painful). The suggestion is then given that this feeling will be used as a bridge to the past and as the therapist counts backwards, the patient will "go back to the very first time you ever had this feeling." When this works, as it usually does, the patient is brought back to some traumatic experience that clearly resembles the object or situation that currently evokes that feeling.

The Corridor of Time

In this technique the hypnotized patient is asked to see himself walking down a long corridor with many closed doors along either side. Each of those doors leads back to some earlier period in his/ her life, and s/he is asked to find the door that leads back to some period in which something happened that caused the symptom to develop. The adult is then asked to open the door and step back in time to see what was happening to the younger self that caused the symptom to develop. Again we learn of a traumatic incident with attendant painful feelings, and again we can see how the symptom protected the patient from experiencing those feelings under similar circumstances.

If one thinks about these five dissimilar sounding techniques, it becomes apparent that they are all really accomplishing the same thing, i.e., focusing the patient's memory on a significant period in his/her personal history. They all usually elicit an emotional response as well. This, I believe, is essentially what is accomplished in more traditional therapies. The main differences are: (1) Traditional therapies use other techniques of inquiry, such as free association, directed associations, dream interpretation, and direct questioning. While these methods also focus on significant periods in the patient's life, they take much longer to get there. (2) Depending upon the theoretical beliefs of the therapist, a specific period in the patient's life will be sought, like infancy, birth, or prior existence. With these hypnotic techniques, the same specific periods *can* be suggested, but usually the patient has the freedom to "return" to the experience that comes to mind without suggestion.

In my experience, some patients respond well to any of the hypnotic techniques; others to only one or two. Those who have trouble visualizing events, for example, do poorly with the corridor of time but might do very well with ego state therapy, which uses more conceptualization than visualization, or with ideomotor signaling, which relies more on a "somatic" response and which, not coincidentally, almost always works well with patients who are having somatic symptoms.

Not uncommonly, after the patient has reported a traumatic incident that seems to have been responsible for having developed the symptom, s/he will declare, "I could have told you about that incident without the use of hypnosis." The patient is probably right. If I had known how to ask the right questions without hypnosis, perhaps I would have received exactly the same information. With hypnosis, however, asking the "right" question becomes very easy. It's essentially, "And what was happening to you at that time in your life?" (The time upon which his memory had been focused by one of the above techniques.)

Why didn't the patient tell me about it before using hypnosis? There's certainly some justification for claiming that I didn't give him ample opportunity because I take such a brief history. How much longer should the history have taken? Another session? Another month? Another year? Frankly, I consider it shamefully extravagant to expend very much time with traditional history-taking if the hypnotic techniques work equally well and more rapidly. The patient has lost nothing by using hypnosis, except his symptoms, and has saved much effort, much money, and much time, during which the symptoms would have continued with all their unpleasant consequences.

But would the patient really have been able to tell me about the traumatic incident without hypnosis? I believe so, and yet many of my patients had seen prior therapists who used traditional methods of inquiry, sometimes for years, without uncovering the traumatic incidents we uncovered, and without improving. Even with my brief history-taking, many patients have expressed what they believed to be the causes of their problems; when this occurred, almost always hypnosis revealed that the causes lay elsewhere.

When the hypnotic techniques reveal a cause other than the one the patient has expected, a common response is, "I knew about that incident before, but I hadn't thought about it in years, and I'd never made a connection between it and my problems. It all makes a lot of sense now." That's one of the lovely things about doing this type of therapy — it does make a lot of sense. And it makes sense to laypersons and professionals alike, with no need for either of them to get involved with complicated theories or almost incomprehensible jargon.

It is interesting to speculate why, if the patient knew about the incident before, s/he had never made the connection between it and the presenting problems. It's certainly possible that there was no connection, as the proponents of infantile conflicts might believe. It's also possible that repression occurred, not for the incident itself but for the significance of the incident. I guess other possibilities also exist, but whatever the reason, the fact remains that the end result is frequently a rapid and apparently permanent relief of the symptom with no substitute symptoms appearing.

Another important question arises, however, "How do you know that the information you obtained through hypnosis is accurate?" I don't. Let me ask, "How do you know that the information you obtained through whatever technique you used is accurate?" If you're honest, I believe you'll have to admit that you don't know, either.

The sad truth is that there is no known method of obtaining information from anyone which guarantees that the seeker will obtain a reliable answer. This applies to Ouiji boards and psychoanalysis, to lie detectors and truth serums, to the violence of a torture chamber and to the sweet gentleness of "But will you respect me in the morning?" It is only through obtaining outside confirmatory evidence that we can be reasonably certain of the facts, and that sort of outside evidence is rarely available to us.

How then do we decide that what a patient is telling us is true?

Mostly through unwarranted assumptions about our ability to do this, although we do use certain standards to bolster our confidence. Those standards are probably no more reliable than our assumptions.

(1) The patient's appearance and manner of presentation will always have some effect on our judgment, but is it really true that "you can't trust anyone over 30," or that shifty-eyed people are always lying, or that a well-dressed, somber, head of state declaring "I'm no crook" is telling the truth? As I've acquired more experience in this profession, I like to think that my judgment about such matters has improved, but I'll never be able to make such discriminations with certainty. As a matter of fact, I'm ashamed to admit that there are still times when I'm inclined to believe a politician.

(2) Does the information seem consistent with our notions of reality? For instance, if a patient says, "My neighbor has this laser machine that puts sexual thoughts in my head," we are not likely to believe it. If he says, "My neighbor undresses in front of her window each night and that puts sexual thoughts in my head," we might.

This is not always reliable, however. For instance, during the 1970s, there were many organizations in Berkeley opposed to the Vietnam war. Members of those organizations would come into my office or those of my colleagues and tell us that the FBI was reading their mail, tapping their phones, infiltrating their organizations, etc. We did not believe them, for our interpretation of reality then was that the FBI was a law-abiding organization and such activities were contrary to the laws of the land. That was our illusion; our patients were probably telling the truth.

(3) Is the patient's information consistent with what he has told us before? Even discounting very clever liars or therapists who do not pay enough attention to pick up inconsistencies, this is not reliable. The most honest of patients may have perceived something incorrectly, or their memories may have been distorted by time, or their unintended fabrication of a story may prove to be extremely consistent, though wrong.

(4) Is the information consistent with our theoretical formulations? The therapist who believes in past lives regressions will believe the

patient who reports having had a chariot accident on the way to the forum; the rest of us will not. Those of us whose theories postulate actual traumatic events as the source of neurotic symptoms will believe the validity of such reports; the psychoanalytically oriented will not, relegating the reports to the role of "screen memories." The analysts who believe that infantile wishes and drives are the source of symptoms will believe their patients' reports of those wishes and drives; others will doubt their validity and/or relevance. So, consistency with a theory seems to be "proof" only to the holder of that particular theory.

(5) Does working with the patient's data produce emotional reaction and lead to improvement? How can we depend on this when we know that no matter what data the patient produces, if s/he and the therapist both believe it to be true, and a few rituals of that particular form of therapy are carried out, improvement will often result? And, of course, it is well-known that inexact or incomplete interpretations also produce emotional reactions and lead to improvement.

To make matters even worse, we must further admit that there's no way of knowing if what we tell our patients is true. Our interventions are based upon the uncertain information that we received from our patients, upon our own associations, our own experiences, our own theories, and our own neuroses. That leaves considerable room for honest error. Anyone who has been present at a case conference has heard how different therapists have found different meanings in the data available, and each of those therapists, in the privacy of his or her own office, would have told the patient a different "truth."

So, although none of us can be certain of the information that we obtain from or offer to our patients, we all continue honoring the validity of our own techniques and continue belittling others' theories and techniques. Perhaps it's only in our disbelief of each other's theories that all of us are finally right. Still, we all have therapeutic failures and triumphs, and the evidence suggests that we all have these in approximately the same proportions.

If the information obtained through hypnotic techniques is no more valid than that obtained through other techniques, there is no good reason to believe that it is less valid either. It can often be obtained more quickly, and that alone is my reason for seeking information in this way.

There may be one important difference, however. There are those researchers who believe that when information is obtained hypnotically, both the patient and the unwary therapist are more convinced of its authenticity. Perhaps those researchers are correct, but it's not uncommon for patients to tell me, "I'm not sure that the information I gave you is accurate." I'm never sure, either, and yet this information, like that obtained by other techniques, usually becomes useful to the patient.

I have alluded to this several times before, but perhaps it's important enough to mention again. If the data that the patient reveals concern a prior life, his birth experience, infantile conflicts, or events occurring later in life, if he and his therapist both believe in the validity of the information, therapeutic gains will often occur. Perhaps it's only necessary that the patient believe it, for on the few occasions that patients of mine have reported prior life experiences, they improved even though I told them that such stories were beyond my belief.

Techniques for Step Four

When it comes to helping the patient understand that the old dangers no longer exist or that there are better ways of protecting himself, there are a number of techniques available. Insight alone helps at times, but not often. Behavioral, cognitive, and strategic techniques may be used, as well as many others. Again, I employ hypnotic techniques (which often employ aspects of those other techniques) simply because they work faster for me.

Generally these hypnotic techniques involve little more than giving patients, or having patients give themselves, clear, rational information and/or options.

We all know that ordinarily such a rational approach is useless. That is, if a patient tells us that his father treated him cruelly and now he feels intimidated around older men, it doesn't help to tell the patient that all old men are not his father and there's no need to feel intimidated around them. When the patient is hypnotized, however, and especially if he has just been remembering the events and to some extent has been experiencing the feelings surrounding those events, such a simple intervention then becomes highly effective.

I cannot explain this effectiveness, and will gladly give others the opportunity to develop their theories about it. I've observed it often, and it still strikes me as being both remarkable and puzzling.

Zilbergeld (1989) offers a possible explanation that deserves serious consideration. He says,

> I believe, without being able to prove anything, that one of the main reasons for the effectiveness of hypnosis is simply the "not-talking set" the patient gets into. When you can't talk, you can listen. When you can talk, you don't listen because you're busy writing your rebuff. I've actually done this a number of times—just told the patient I would like to tell him something which he needed to understand and that I didn't want him to interrupt or respond in any way that day—and as far as I can tell the listening and the acceptance are quite high. Much higher than just telling them something in the ordinary way. As high as formal hypnosis? I have no way of knowing for sure, but I think so.

Let Zilbergeld's technique serve as my first illustration of why I don't believe that hypnosis is necessary.

General Principles of Brief Therapy

In addition to the principles involved in the theory and techniques about which I have been writing so far, there are a few other generalities that apply to virtually all forms of brief therapy:

(1) The therapist must be very active during the sessions. By being active, I mean that the therapist must actively inquire, clarify, and comment. He cannot maintain the "silent mirror" attitude that long-

term therapists advocate but which so many patients find intolerable and of no help at all.

He must be actively empathic, not only for the sorrows and setbacks that a patient relates, but for the joys and successes as well. When a patient has attempted what to him is a scary new effort to improve his life, and has succeeded, the therapist's honest display of pleasure and words of congratulations do much to encourage further efforts.

At times the therapist should actively "prescribe" new approaches to problems rather than play a therapeutic game of "let's see if I can get you to think about doing what I think you should do." Here's a simple example taken from a 15-minute session that had originally been scheduled as a medication follow-up.

The patient was a 58-year-old businessman, hardworking and successful. He had had a series of panic attacks, but had been free of those symptoms for several months, since being started on trazodone. At this "medication" visit he told me that he found no pleasure in life anymore. He was okay while working, "but this weekend when it was raining and I couldn't get out, I had nothing to do and I was miserable."

A few moments later I learned that his wife had always been full of life and had kept the whole family busy and entertained; however, for the last two years arthritis had severely impaired her activities, and now he was bored. He resented it, and recently had spoken out in anger to her; then he felt guilty "because I know I shouldn't feel that way."

Finally, he revealed that he resented losing the good sex life that they had had, but he had lost his interest in sex because he never knew if this movement or that would hurt her arthritis. She had been trying, unsuccessfully, to be seductive with him, and was feeling hurt because no matter what she tried he displayed no interest.

I told him that it was perfectly normal to feel angry about losing so much, it wasn't wrong at all to have those feelings, and they *should* be expressed. He'd already seen that if he expressed them to his wife, that made him feel guilty because he knew it wasn't her fault. I then told him how to get the feelings out by writing an extremely angry letter that no one would see (this will be described in more detail later). I suggested that he let his wife know *why* he wasn't interested in sex. At the very least this would make her feel better, because then she'd realize that his abstinence was a sign of his concern for her, not an indication of lost love. Furthermore, if the two of them talked about it, they almost certainly could come up with one position or another that wouldn't hurt her.

Finally, we discussed the value of finding new at-home hobbies to keep him busy, not only to help things now, but in preparation for retirement, which was not too far away. This discussion led him to remember hobbies that he'd enjoyed in the past and that he'd like to try again.

This one 15-minute session, extended to 20 minutes, proved to be immensely helpful to him. Without the activity on my part, he could have spent many hours trying to come up with similar solutions.

From a theoretical standpoint, it could be argued that my supplying him with solutions was wrong, because this diminished his independence. From a practical standpoint, counterarguments could be advanced: (a) He could independently accept or reject the suggestions; if he accepted them, then he, not I, would be the one doing the work involved. (b) If a 58-year-old man has depended on his wife for many years to find entertainment for him, no 20-minute session is likely to make him a helluva lot more dependent. (c) As a matter of observation, many patients, once given a model to solve problems in one situation, can easily transpose that model into many other situations.

(2) The therapist must clarify the symptoms and consolidate them where possible. When symptoms are consolidated there are fewer with which to work, and termination can be achieved more quickly. The consolidation also gives the patient the helpful realization that there are not as many things out of control as s/he originally believed; there are only one or a few, manifest in different ways. For example, in one of the cases that I'll be presenting, the patient complained of being a pathological liar and losing friends because of that, of sabotaging good jobs and losing them because of that, and of acceding to his mother's excessive demands and suffering a variety of losses because

of that. These three separate complaints were successfully consolidated into one, self-destructive behavior.

(3) The therapist must keep the patient's focus on the symptoms about which he is complaining and not let irrelevant material intrude. The question of what is irrelevant is not easily answered. What initially appears to be irrelevant may eventually be seen as having a significant bearing on the work being done. What initially sounds like an important new aspect of the problem under study may turn out to be an interesting but wasteful digression.

The more freely the therapist allows the patient to say whatever comes to mind, the greater the chance of gaining more and more relevant data, but at terrible expense, for this nondirected approach also guarantees a number of excursions that are nothing more than fruitless detours.

My own preference is to obtain a clear understanding of the presenting symptom(s) and to obtain a very brief personal history. The personal history may include little more than what it was like to grow up in the patient's family; what his relations were like with parents, siblings, and classmates; how he did in school; and what he did after graduation from high school. By brief, I mean that all of the above can be obtained in the first hour, often with enough time left over to introduce the patient to hypnosis, if hypnosis is to be used.

It has been my experience that after obtaining the above information the search for the traumatic incidents gives all the additional history that is needed for therapy. In some cases, if the symptom is rather circumscribed and does not pervade the patient's whole life, the only history I seek is that of the symptom itself.

(4) The therapist must be able to move easily from one technique to another if the first technique is not working well. This is not limited to moving from one hypnotic technique to another, but includes moving from insight-oriented therapy to supportive therapy or pharmacotherapy and back again. It includes using behavior therapy, cognitive therapy, strategic therapy, etc., and going from one to the other, depending on what problems are coming up and what responses are being obtained.

6 | CLINICAL CASES

IN THIS CHAPTER, I will give case illustrations of these principles. Since I believe that the principles are more important than the specific techniques, the illustrations from my own cases will all be brief. The nonhypnotic cases, taken from other authors, will also be brief; I apologize to those authors in advance for not displaying their skills to greater advantage. When the therapist follows these principles and combines them with the hypnotic techniques described or with any other fast uncovering techniques that are more comfortable to the therapist, then symptoms can be analyzed rapidly and patients improve quickly.

Although I have previously stated that one cannot always believe the clinical reports of an author, I will offer clinical reports anyway, for I have found no better method of illustrating the principles involved.

A Patient with Multiple Symptoms;
Symptom Analysis, Hypnotic Techniques

My first case, one that was treated using some of the hypnotic techniques previously described, shows in clear fashion how symptom analysis can be accomplished rapidly and effectively in a patient with multiple symptoms. It is merely a matter of taking them one by one if they are discrete symptoms, appear at different stages of the therapy, or for any other reason cannot be consolidated into one or two symptoms.

When this patient was first seen she was 31 years old. She was married, was pleased with her family and her job, denied any external stressors, and said that this should be the happiest time of her life. But it wasn't. On that first visit she expressed two major complaints: depression since the death of her father two years earlier, and the inability to have fun because she felt compelled to stay busy doing "useful" things all the time.

Because I judged her to be clinically depressed, she was started on an antidepressant. I explained ego state therapy to her and induced a hypnotic state, but did not start any uncovering work during that first induction. Obtaining her history, starting the medication, and introducing her to hypnosis occupied the first two sessions.

In the third session, using ego state therapy, in which the "different parts of the personality" can be spoken to, I asked to speak with that part that caused her to feel the need to stay busy all of the time. I learned that this part originated when she was eight or nine. She had been outside playing with friends when her mother called her into the house and informed her that now she was old enough to help with the housework. She stayed in, helped her mother, and received abundant praise for the good work that she did.

It seemed likely that the "part" was keeping her busy doing things as an attempt to help her reexperience the pleasure that she had obtained from her mother's praise. The part confirmed this. While she remained in hypnosis, I commented that good work is certainly one way to obtain praise, but that it can also cause difficulties in that it takes time away from enjoying her family, her friends, and the many other activities that would be available to her. Having fun and sharing that fun with those she cares about would almost certainly be another way to obtain the approval of others, and just having time to relax would make her a calmer, happier person whom her family could enjoy more.

During the fourth session she reported that she was feeling less driven but offered three new complaints: (1) She was feeling bored with too little to do; (2) she was afraid of many activities (riding in boats and going in cars were her two main examples); and (3) she saw sex as an obligation and had only enjoyed it three times in her whole life.

Without using hypnosis, I spoke of the opportunity she now had to find interesting new things to do, inquired about her fears of certain activities (telling her nothing that I recognized as being therapeutic), and learned that she was not ready to discuss the sexual problem at this time.

At session five she reported that she had had a very good week. She had realized that she could entertain herself and had not felt bored since. She had become more assertive toward her mother, who had been intruding into her child-rearing activities, and toward her husband, who hadn't been helping enough around the house. She attributed this new assertiveness to the fact that she had learned that pleasing others was not the only way to find satisfaction in life.

At the sixth session she reported that she was feeling very good! Now she wanted to work on her sexual problem because the other problems were no longer bothering her. There was a moderate amount of resistance during this session. She wouldn't speak under hypnosis but by nodding or shaking her head she indicated that her sexual problem had started at age 19, when she had had intercourse for the first time. Something bad had happened then, and the ego state that was stopping her from enjoying sex was trying to protect her from experiencing the same sort of trauma again. This ego state was willing to let me know about it, but it didn't want her to remember it.

At the seventh session, under hypnosis, she did tell me verbally how angry she had been the first time she had had intercourse. She had been with a man whom she described as "no good," one who didn't care about her at all and who only wanted sex. He had talked her into it despite her initial strong objections. She said that her bottled-up anger had prevented her from enjoying sex ever since.

I had her go through a hypnotic technique called "silent abreaction," in which the patient imagines herself expressing all her rage at the one who engendered it, then relaxing, then expressing the rage again, relaxing, and repeating this process until most of the feelings had subsided. I then elaborated on the differences between her husband and that first man, with my comments heavily favoring the husband.

At her eighth session she was feeling so good that she wanted to discontinue the antidepressant. I advised that it was probably premature, but said that if she really wished to try I'd go along. She said that she had had excellent sex once with her husband since the last visit, and had come to the realization that she had often rejected her husband's attentions because she felt that those attentions were always intended to lead to sex. She now saw that often his attempts to hug or kiss her were only signs of affection.

At the ninth session she said she was feeling fine. Her sex life was now described as "wonderful," her husband's responses were highly gratifying, and her general self-concept had greatly improved. She felt ready to terminate, and I agreed, having spent a total of nine sessions to resolve a number of different symptoms.

This patient returned to my office five and a half years later because her depression had returned, as depressions are wont to do. She reported that all of the other problems were still gone. She again responded very quickly to antidepressant medication.

Discussion

This case illustrates a number of the issues discussed in the preceding chapters:

It demonstrates that early childhood and adolescent experiences serve as an adequate explanation for symptom formation. Other therapists working with other theories would have found other explanations that came from earlier times in her life, and in all probability they would have obtained equally helpful results. From this I again conclude that we can neither judge the validity of a theory on the basis of results obtained nor believe that infantile fantasies must be uncovered to obtain significant and long lasting improvements.

In dealing with the symptom of having to stay busy all the time, we see an illustration of the corollary to the trauma theory. The relief of this symptom occurred quickly once she understood its origin and learned that there was a better way to obtain what she wanted (the corollary to finding a better way to protect oneself). Not only was this one symptom relieved, but there was a widespread effect; i.e., once she understood that it was no longer necessary to go to extremes to please others, she was able to become more assertive. I cannot account for her no longer fearing certain activities, unless that was also part of her new assertiveness.

The relief of her sexual difficulties was, I believe, partly attributable to the silent and symbolic release of her anger; however, I suspect that it was also clearly related to her realization that "the old danger no longer exists," i.e., her husband would not make her feel the humiliation and anger that the first man had evoked.

That realization probably came about through her acceptance of the simple, rational explanation I offered about the differences between her husband and the first man. This tack is often effective when the patient is under hypnosis, even though such explanations fall on deaf ears otherwise. With this realization, there was not only complete removal of her sexual symptom but also broader improvement, in that she could recognize her husband as a loving spouse and herself as a lovable person.

As illustrated here, the benefits obtained by these techniques can be long lasting. Five and a half years are hardly a lifetime, so we do not know if the benefits are permanent, but if they have lasted that long, they might be, particularly since the changes she made are so gratifying that there is bound to be a great deal of positive reinforcement.

I do not know for sure that these long enduring or permanent changes are typical, for I do not have a system to follow most of my patients after discharge. However, these results do seem typical for most of the patients who have returned to see me for some new problem three to five years after our original termination, and it certainly fits with the findings of Nicholson and Berman (1983) that the data obtained at follow-up add little to the information obtained at the end of therapy (in regard to the quality and duration of improvement). In only one of my cases did the original symptoms return after symptom analysis; this was a phobia which I reported as a successful cure in *Trauma, Trance, and Transformation* (p. 106). In all other instances, returning patients have reported that the original symptoms have not reappeared. Of course, it's entirely possible that patients who did not return had symptoms that did.

Nonhypnotic techniques certainly could have been used in this case. For example, Zilbergeld (personal communication) obtains very similar historical data without the use of hypnosis—or at least without a formal hypnotic induction. He merely asks a whole series of questions about when the symptom started and what was going on in the patient's life at that time. Then, after getting answers to the questions, the whole purpose of which is to get the patient focused on that period, he asks, "Could you allow your mind to go back to that time just before you first experienced . . . (the symptom)? Good, now just observe what happens, and take all the time that you need."

Does the lack of a "hypnotic induction" mean that we do not have hypnosis? Since no one can adequately define hypnosis, that question is impossible to answer. However, let's look at some reports. We'll start with Zilbergeld's, in which he obtains the same sort of data that I do "without hypnosis." Then, remember what I said on page 00 about Cheek's method of doing ideomotor signaling; he found that inducing hypnosis before starting the finger signals was not necessary, but as he asked the questions, the patient seemed to go into a hypnotic state. Finally, let me quote briefly from Budman and Gurman (1988, p. 88) (I'll offer more of this same quotation later): "As they begin to recall and search for significant details, many people take on the glazed, distant expression typical of those in an eyes-open trance state."

This is intriguing. Does it mean that it's wasteful to take the time to do a formal hypnotic induction? Would merely asking for very detailed descriptions of what was going on at some certain time do the same thing? I don't think so, for a formal induction need not take more than one-half to two minutes, and asking such detailed questions takes me longer. Does it mean that those therapists who do ask detailed questions obtain a hypnotic state or a state closely resembling hypnosis? If they only realized this and then asked the question, "And what was happening about that time that caused the symptom to develop?", could they then get the answer? I don't know for sure, but that's pretty close to what Zilbergeld does.

So we see that it's not necessary to use hypnosis to get the information we want. It's not necessary to use hypnosis to have the patient accept the explanations we offer, for rational therapy, cognitive therapy, or just getting the patient into a "listening, not-talking" mode might do the same. The hypnotic technique of "silent abreaction" is not necessary to dissipate angry feelings, for there are certainly other techniques to do that, some of which will be described in the next section. Despite the fact that all of these things can be accomplished without hypnosis, I find that the hypnotic techniques work better and faster for me, and so I continue to use them.

One further note on this first case: Although this patient's obsessive-compulsive symptoms were readily cleared by symptom analysis, as they have been with a number of other patients who displayed relatively mild symptoms, this technique has not worked in my patients with severe obsessive-compulsive symptoms. It's possible that in those cases the biological factor is too great to be overcome by this method.

A Patient with Low Self-Esteem

In Chapter 2 I mention Gustafson's "Case of Bulimia" (1986, p. 230–235). In that case he successfully treated a young woman who had begun failing at all she was doing, despite earlier having been a high achiever. The patient had also become very self-denigrating, was apparently having sexual problems that were not clearly specified but had to do with the necessity of "keeping an even keel," and had bulimia of six years' duration. During the course of therapy he discovered, among other things, that one of the reasons she was maintaining her symptoms was that she believed it was necessary in order to keep the family stabilized. She felt that her mother needed to feel important and that the only way that could happen would be for her to remain dependent on the mother.

I suggested a hypothetical way the case might have been handled had it been treated with symptom analysis. My hypothesis included the belief that the therapist could probably uncover a series of traumas in which the patient had been made to feel badly because she was too successful at things; her becoming unsuccessful was a symptom which served to protect her from the recurrence of those bad feelings. This case of my own bears definite similarities to Gustafson's, except that my patient did not have bulimia.

The patient was a 40-year-old professional woman who entered therapy because of what she first described as depression. She then redefined her symptom as a persistent feeling of unhappiness because of excessive self-doubt and self-criticism. She knew that she had been successful and competent, but that knowledge did little to relieve her feelings. She had had two prior courses of therapy elsewhere, each lasting about a year, but her problems persisted.

She described her father as a narcissistic, unloving man who had seen her as a child as "only being in the way." Her mother was constantly depressed, critical of herself and of the patient. The patient had always felt "not good enough" and had repetitively sought the approval of men who were critical and rejecting. Surprisingly, but happily, her second marriage was to a loving and supportive man.

Because this patient had been hypnotized before elsewhere and had already heard about ego state therapy, it was not necessary to take time explaining either to her. We were able to start an analysis of her symptoms during that first visit.

The "part" that caused the patient to have excessive self-doubt and self-criticism developed when she was about two. She said that at that time she was feeling alone and frightened and was afraid that there was something wrong with her. She had the feeling that her parents would be even more displeased with her if she were happy.

It seemed to me, then, that the "part" was protecting her in two ways: It kept her unhappy, which would prevent the parents from becoming even more displeased, and it might, through harsh criticism, motivate her to correct whatever was "very much wrong with her." The part agreed that this was true.

While she was still under hypnosis, I pointed out that there was a better way to protect herself from being "not good enough," and that was to use gentler, more constructive criticism. I elaborated on this theme, using her own experience that children learn more quickly in a nonhostile environment, where they are praised for their accomplishments rather than criticized harshly for their failures.

At the second session, one week later, she reported that there had been no change and that she was feeling discouraged. As we discussed her discouragement after only one session, I learned that, when she had seen another therapist who had also used hypnosis, he had made some very happy predictions for her that had not come true. Her bitter disappointment over that was being transferred to this new situation. After we discussed this a bit, she was willing to continue.

We used the "corridor of time" technique, in which the patient sees herself walking down a long hallway with doors leading to earlier periods in her life. She finds the door that leads back to that period in which something happened that caused the symptom to develop. This took her back again to the age of two. This time I asked her, as an adult, to reassure the "little girl" of her worth, explaining to that little girl that, instead of there being something wrong with her, there must have been something sadly wrong with her parents. Perhaps the parents had had psychological problems that prevented them from giving her the love and affection she deserved; if that were true, it really wasn't their fault, but still, they had treated her tragically, and there must be a great deal of anger about that. She was given the opportunity to discharge her pent-up anger.

The third and fourth sessions consisted mostly of descriptions of the different ways in which she was feeling progressively better, plus discussions of some of the realistic problems in her daily life and ways she could deal with them more effectively. During the fourth session we used hypnosis to reinforce some of the concepts we had previously discussed: She no longer needed to protect herself from her parents' displeasure by being unhappy; allowing herself to be happy would now serve her better; positive approaches were more likely to lead her to any improvements she sought so she could use those instead of the harsh criticisms.

At the fifth and final session, two weeks later, she happily announced that she was doing very well now and would return only if she had further problems. That was about 18 months ago; she has not returned.

Discussion

I had hypothesized that Gustafson's case could have been treated in this manner. He, if he chose to do so, could hypothesize that my case could have been treated equally well via the systemic perspective that he used. I would have no disagreement at all. Certainly, both families were dysfunctional, and it should be easy to find, in either case, the ways in which the patients' symptoms were protective of their respective parents or of themselves. He chose one perspective, I chose the other; there is no reason to believe that either way is better. I am in full agreement with Milton Erickson, "Do anything that works."

It is interesting to note that the excessive self-criticism was a symptom designed to motivate this patient to become better and thus to protect her from the bad feelings of not being good enough. When discussing cognitive therapy in an earlier chapter, I remarked that this was a frequently found explanation for the negative view of the self, one of the elements of the negative triad that cognitive therapists find in depressed patients. (The other two elements are a negative view of the present and a negative view of the future.)

Another brief case presentation demonstrates how this particular symptom occurred in somewhat similar circumstances.

Another Case of Low Self-Esteem;
Symptom Analysis with Hypnotic Techniques

This patient was a 34-year-old divorcée who worked for an electronics firm in an administrative position. She entered therapy because of "low self-esteem." She told me that she had always received little affection but many derogatory comments from her father. Although she had always felt close to her mother, her mother had done little to help build her confidence in herself. Additionally, she had always been taller than her peers, so she had always felt odd around them.

When she had started dating she was always "too demanding," wanted to go steady too soon, and scared the boys away. (I imagined, but did not comment, that these symptomatic behaviors were attempts to reassure her that she was valued, but as symptoms usually do, they failed to fulfill their intended purpose.)

She had married when 22, but after seven months her husband left her for another woman. She had been seeing her current boyfriend for over a year but realized that she was too demanding of him and was afraid that he, too, would also be driven away.

Obtaining that history and introducing her to hypnosis occupied the first session.

In the second session we used ego state therapy. She named the part that caused her to feel the low self-esteem "Big Lummox." This part developed when she was ten and was being criticized constantly by her father. It was trying to help her. It believed that its own constant criticisms would make her work harder to improve herself and thus become more acceptable to other people. This part was able to understand rather quickly that the opposite effect was occurring and agreed to be gentler and more constructive in its efforts to help her improve herself. The patient renamed the part "Friend."

At the third visit she reported a "remarkable change." She was feeling very good about herself and was getting along much better with her father, her boyfriend, and all the people at work. She found that she was no longer demanding of them, and they were all responding to her in a much more positive way. We used hypnosis to reinforce the gains that she had made and agreed that we would terminate therapy at that point, but that she should return at any time if she felt it would be useful to do so. She has made no further demands for therapy.

Client-Centered Therapy

Rogers (1977) presented "The Case of Mary Jane Tilden" as an example of his work utilizing this form of therapy. It's interesting to note the similarities between Gustafson's case, the two that I just presented, and this one. The therapeutic techniques are clearly different, yet all of them yielded good results.

In her first statement to Rogers the patient says, "It is a long story. I can't find myself. Everything I do seems to be wrong. I can't get on with people. If there is any criticism or anyone says anything about me I just can't take it. When I had a job, if anyone said anything critical, it just crumpled me." By the end of the first session, Rogers had collected 24 significant feelings, 23 of which were various ways of saying that she had low self-esteem. The 24th was, "I guess I'll come back" (for a second session).

The first eight sessions were devoted primarily to talking about current feelings and events. I'll now quote an excerpt from session nine (pp. 215–216).

> She realizes that she is always dissatisfied with anything she does—her job or any other undertaking. Part of the reason for this is that she feels she never achieves more than a mediocre standard, and this she cannot accept, but "I've got to face it, it just was." She is convinced that whatever she might do, it just would not work out well. She is convinced she is a moron because she can follow a teacher, but can do nothing on her own initiative. She continues:
> S154. I've either been afraid to trust my own ability and afraid to go out on my own or something. That's just a habit, that was just sort of a habit that I formed. I mean, relying on my teachers, really, just groping at meanings.

C154. As long as someone else was in charge, why, it was O.K., you got along, but when it came to a question of doing something on your own ability, in your own direction, to choose and manage, why you don't have any luck.

S155. That's right.

C155. It boils down again to what's come up in some other ways, doesn't it, that you just trust others (she cries) and believe in them, but belief in yourself, that's just impossible.

S156. Yes, that's just the idea. Don't you think that somewhere along the line something would happen — something might turn up that — it's a very funny situation.

C156. You feel that something should have turned up to give you that confidence in yourself.

S157. Yes. It should. I should have thought of it or something. (Crying.) When you watch a little child he seems to — well, he seems to want to get out on his own, he seems to be happy when he can get out.

C157. You feel very deeply about it, that even a little child feels so much pleasure in standing on his own two feet.

S158. Well, possibly being — oh, dear, here comes the rainstorm. (Cries.)

C158. They say the rain makes things grow.

S159. Very aptly put. (Long pause, crying.) Well, perhaps being at home has something to do with it — I mean my mother has always been very good to me. She had a miserable childhood, her parents never paid any attention to her, then she tried to make up for it, and that way it didn't affect the others because they didn't accept it, but I accepted what she did for me and I just took it for granted, and it made me more reliant on her, really.

C159. You feel that because of some of her very real needs that — she did a great deal for you and you accepted it and depended on her.

S160. That's right.

C160. You stood on her two feet.

S161. That's right. Now my little sister, she isn't that way, she's in the adolescent stage right now; she is branching out for herself, I mean she just doesn't like it. She wants to be consulted about everything that she does, and everything like that. Well, my sister isn't letting it affect her. I know she feels in her own heart that it's right, and I used to wonder about that, I mean every time that I did something I used to think, well, maybe she is right, maybe I should do the way she does, and then I switch over, and I wouldn't stand up on my own two feet.

C161. You watched your sister stand out against some of your mother's thinking, and some of your mother's requests, but when you were in that stage you couldn't—you didn't feel it was quite right to stand up against her on any of those issues . . .

While this does not clearly describe a traumatic event, the patient's accepting what her mother did for her could be seen from Gustafson's systemic perspective as an attempt to protect the mother or from my perspective as a probable attempt to protect herself from whatever dangers the patient feared might occur if she did not accept her mother's help. My assumption is partly reinforced by Rogers' comment, "You didn't feel it was quite right to stand up against her."

At the next session the patient reported more progress and was thinking of taking a different job. Rogers says, "She is sure her family would disapprove of the work. . . . However, she looks back on the decisions they have made for her, and does not have much confidence in them." (She realizes the danger of their disapproval is no longer a great threat.)

The theme of no longer fearing danger (to the mother? to herself?) continues in the tenth session, where she also talks about just living for pats on the back from her parents (corollary to the trauma theory), and comes to the understanding that there are better ways to gain satisfaction (corollary to finding better ways to protect oneself).

The case was terminated by mutual agreement after the eleventh session. Follow-up showed that the patient did well for most of a year, had some relapse after a boyfriend seemed to belittle her, and then showed improvement again, but of unknown duration.

Thus we see examples of how similar cases can be treated in very dissimilar fashion; however, in each the principles of the trauma theory and therapy based upon it can be found. Hypnotic techniques simply make therapy easier and faster.

Play Therapy

Bornstein (1977) presents the case of a child with a school and separation phobia treated with play therapy. The patient was a boy $5^{1}/_{2}$ years old, who had had his phobias for over two years. His sister was born when he was $3^{1}/_{4}$.

This patient showed great anger at his mother and became violent, panic-stricken, and clinging when she wanted to leave without taking him along. His play during the first session "revealed at once the experiences that had led to his phobia and thus betrayed the meaning of his symptoms."

In that session he built a hospital with a lady department, a baby department, and a men's department. A lonely boy of four was seated all by himself. A fire broke out and all the babies were burned to death. He rescued all the women who had no babies, but the one whom he had addressed as "Mommy" was killed in the fire.

Here we have play therapy used as a means of uncovering the traumatic event, the child's sense of abandonment by his mother when she went to the hospital to give birth to his sister. His symptom of clinging to her or becoming panic-stricken if she attempted to leave can be seen clearly as a means of protecting himself from reexperiencing the painful feelings of abandonment.

As Bornstein states, "The patient had successfully concealed from himself the affect of sadness which evidently had been too painful for him to bear. He had replaced it by his aggressive and tyrannical demands to which he later reacted with his phobic symptoms" (p. 111). Later, Bornstein states that the symptoms also protected him from the anxiety that his rage had destroyed his mother.

At this state of the analysis we can already see the first three steps of therapy based upon the trauma theory: (1) uncovering of the traumatic events, (2) recognition of the painful feelings they created, and (3) understanding of how the symptoms served to protect the patient from experiencing those feelings again. Had the therapist chosen to do so, she probably could have applied the fourth step (letting him see that the dangers no longer exist or that there are better ways of protecting himself), and the case may have terminated successfully and quickly.

Indeed, Bornstein offered four possible actions she then could have taken. The first was interpretation of the various motivations for his aggression. Of the four possibilities, I'd expect this to be the least likely to be effective.

The second was for the therapist to participate in the play and encourage expression of his hostility. "This catharsis might soon lead to a diminishing of his phobia." If so, I'd see it as a result of his realizing that the danger of his destructive rage was gone, so he no longer needed the symptom to protect himself from the anxiety about destroying his mother. This, per se, would not provide protection against the fear of being abandoned again, but perhaps the repetitious playing of the event would serve as a desensitizing technique in which the fantasied abandonment recurred and nothing bad happened.

The third possibility was, "We might devalue the conflict by reassuring the child that such conflicts are frequent, natural, and understandable." Basically this would be using rational therapy to help the patient understand that a danger no longer existed.

The fourth possibility was that the therapist might take a criticizing attitude, by appealing to the child's desire to grow up and not to indulge in such infantile phobic mechanisms. To me, this would involve helping him find better ways of protecting himself.

Bornstein says of these four approaches, "They all might lead to a quick disappearance of the symptom." She chose not to use any of them, however, because she wanted to produce "ego change," and thus the therapy went on much longer than was necessary to relieve the poor child and his family of what must have been a hellish situation.

I won't go into the several specific reasons why I believe the prolongation of therapy was of dubious value, but I will repeat that numerous studies have shown that long-term therapy is no better than short-term.

An Adult with a Phobia;
Symptom Analysis with Hypnotic Techniques

I do not see children, except on rare occasions, so I have no cases that are quite the equivalent of Bornstein's. I wish to present this next case, however, because some of the principles will apply anyway.

This patient entered treatment specifically for a phobia. At the first session he told me that his phobia had been present for about 20 years but had been getting much worse for the past six or seven. He was afraid of doctors, dentists, and hospitals; the symptom was so severe that he had fainted on several occasions when he had to see a doctor, and once even when he had gone to visit a friend in the hospital. During the first session this history was obtained and he was introduced to hypnosis.

At the second session we used the ideomotor technique, in which "automatic" finger signals can be used to answer questions that cannot be readily answered by conscious intent. This indicated that something had occurred around age nine that caused his phobia to develop. We then used age regression to take him back to age nine. Apparently he had had an anaphylactic reaction and had been hospitalized. He had been very frightened about what had happened to his body, as it became swollen in various places, partly blocking his breathing. While enduring a number of painful treatments, he had felt not only frightened but also deserted. It turned out that his mother was in another hospital, and his father could not stay with him because he had to visit her, too.

I had the "adult" part of his reassure the "child" part that he no longer had to be frightened. Doctors, nurses, and hospitals were described as places of safety and healing, to protect him from dangerous illness and to relieve painful conditions. This analysis of his symptom and application of step number four (the reassurance that the old danger no longer existed) occupied session two.

He returned for a final visit a few weeks later. He reported that he had gone to a doctor once in the interim and had had no trouble. I hypnotized him and had him visualize himself going into a hospital;

even though I deliberately made the scene unpleasant and bloody, he felt nothing more than very mild discomfort. Previously he would become anxious just thinking about being in the lobby of a hospital. This type of visualization generally serves as an excellent predictor of how the patient will feel in a real life situation in the future.

Another Adult with a Phobia; Symptom Analysis with Hypnotic Techniques

A 45-year-old man came into the office complaining of a phobia of crowds. This phobia had started four years previously while he was in a crowded restaurant. He knew of no precipitating events but thought that it might be the result of an ugly incident that had occurred 15 years before. Apparently through no fault of his own, he had been the center of a riot at a football game. Several of his friends who came to his aid were injured, two of them permanently.

Admitting that this could be the source of his phobia but proposing that we look for other possible sources, I used the corridor of time, and he went back to the age of five. He saw himself lying on the kitchen floor, looking out through the screen door at a dangerous dog from his neighborhood and feeling very comfortable and safe.

Seeing no relationship between that scene and his symptom, I asked how he felt about crowds at that time in his life. He responded, "There were no crowds in that little town," and then his whole body tensed, his breathing became rapid, he started shaking, and said, "Yes, oh, yes, now I know." He described a terrifying incident.

It was Veterans Day in his home town, and his mother had taken him to the local cemetery to put some flowers on the graves of men who had died in World War II. A small two-seater airplane was flying low, dropping flowers into the cemetery. The plane struck a tree, and one of the occupants was impaled upon a branch and died screaming as the plane erupted into flames beneath him. A large crowd gathered to watch this disaster. As horrified as he was, the small boy could not divert his eyes from the scene.

I offered a simple suggestion, "Now that you know why you felt frightened in a crowd, perhaps you'll never have to have that fear again." He left the office shaken.

When he came back the next week, he reported that he'd tried going into a crowded place only once, but it hadn't been bad. He told me that now he understood why he felt so uncomfortable when his family had asked that he take them to an air show, and why he had refused to park any closer than a few miles from it. He promised to expose himself to crowds in the near future and to call me back if he was still having trouble. I contacted him by phone a year later, and he was doing fine.

Discussion

These two phobia cases illustrate several points. The trauma theory is easily discernible in them, as it was in the case presented by Bornstein. When the fourth step of therapy, letting the patient understand that the old dangers no longer exist, is undertaken promptly after discovering the source of the trauma, the case can usually be terminated quickly thereafter with good results. Finally, although many, possibly the majority of short-term therapists now use desensitizing techniques to treat a phobia, these cases demonstrate that symptom analysis can also be highly effective. In some cases it may even be more effective, for once patients understand what the old dangers were, they can more easily give up the symptom that they had been using to protect themselves from those dangers.

Gestalt Therapy

Laura Perls (1977) presents "The Case of Walter," which I will now examine briefly. Perls describes this 47-year-old European Jewish refugee as follows:

> He is dissatisfied and in a dull way unhappy with nearly everything in his life. He is not so much complaining as berating himself for being such a failure in business, in social contacts, in family life. He

postpones everything that is not strictly routine, minor business phone calls as well as major decisions. He dreads meeting people, has to break his head for something to say, feels awkward and self-conscious. He is afraid of losing old business connections and convinced of his inability to make new ones. In spite of all these obvious limitations and self-recriminations, the patient is not unsuccessful in business, makes a comfortable living as an agent for some foreign business concerns, has kept the same accounts for many years, and is appreciated for his reliability and foresight. His children love him. He also has a small number of good friends. He gets great enjoyment from being out in the open, in contact with nature. But this more positive information was not available at the beginning of his therapy. (p. 243)

This patient was seen twice weekly for four months, once weekly in group sessions for ten months, and was still in group therapy when the case was reported. He was said to be doing very well. Perls summarizes his treatment:

It took a number of months to make him realize that what he felt was not, as he maintained, "nothing," but was rather discomfort, tension, impatience, irritability, distrust, apprehension; that what he did also was not "nothing," but was rather pulling himself together, suspending animation, waiting for something to be over, whether it be a business meeting, an argument with his wife, or a therapy session.

Listening to his voice, the patient found to his surprise not only that he sounded like his father (a fact that he had always known) but also, particularly when he was berating and belittling himself, that he sounded like his mother having an argument with his father. The suspended animation attitude was thus revealed as a most adequate support for the child to keep out of an unmanageable and unsolvable conflict. The ensuing desensitization led to the introjection of and identification with that very conflict, and in turn to an externalization, which transformed every contact situation into a potential threat. (p. 244)

Here again we see the trauma theory in action. The traumas were the arguments between his parents. His suspended animation served "as a most adequate support for the child to keep out of an unmanageable and unsolvable conflict." (It protected him from the painful feelings caused by the conflict.) This analysis of the symptoms was obtained by focusing on the patient's voice, attitudes, movements, postures, etc.

The therapeutic portion of the treatment consisted of "awareness experiments and exercises" to loosen up his voice and his movements, plus focusing on his feelings, which he was then encouraged to endure rather than avoid. From my perspective, this means that he was taught, by a very slow desensitization technique, that it was *safe* to speak out, move with animation, and even endure painful feelings. (See, the dangers you feared will not hurt you.)

We know of 112 visits, plus an unspecified number of ongoing group visits. This certainly cannot be called brief therapy but it was effective, accomplishing all four of the therapeutic steps of which I've been speaking without recourse to hypnosis.

An Inhibited Woman;
Symptom Analysis with Hypnotic Techniques

The patient I'll now present was not nearly as inhibited as Perls', so any comparison between the two must take that into account. She was in her late thirties, very tall, strikingly attractive, and so carefully coiffed and made up that she looked like a model without anorexia. She had a panic disorder and was responding well to medical management of that disease.

She complained that she was distraught because she had decisions to make. Her husband wanted to move to a community near the one in which her parents lived. She was afraid to give up her current home in which she felt so comfortable. Her children didn't want to move, and she was afraid that she'd "lose" them if she agreed to move. She was afraid that she'd lose her husband if she didn't, and that if she didn't move close to her parents they couldn't help her "grow up into an adult" before they died. She very rarely made demands on anyone or argued with them because she feared they'd get angry and desert her if she did.

I felt that the primary inhibiting factor in her life was the fear that she would be deserted if she asserted herself in any way. She agreed to using hypnosis, and we did ego state therapy to understand the part that gave her this fear.

The responses she gave indicated that this part had developed when she was very young, three or four. At that time she was feeling lonely and frightened. She was alone, wanted her mother, but her mother wouldn't come to her. She concluded that her mother was staying away because she had been bad. This traumatic incident, which may have been a metaphor for a number of similar incidents, gave her very painful feelings, and to protect herself from experiencing them again she had become overly compliant.

While she remained in the hypnotic state, I pointed out the obvious: that even if her mother had punished her when she was bad by making her stay in a room by herself, she really had not been abandoned, for her mother did come back to her. That's what happens when people who love one another get angry. There's a brief period of unpleasantness and then they are close again. This theme was elaborated.

She returned two weeks later, reporting that in the interim she had had a big argument with her husband, had stood her ground nicely, and everything had turned out well in the end. For the first time that she could remember, she felt like she was an adult and could see how childish he was being. She was now preparing to tell her mother of her displeasure about the fact that her mother was planning to leave all 20 acres of the land on which the patient had grown up to her sister. The patient had a strong sentimental attachment to that property and wanted to inherit at least a small portion of it. She had only the slightest concern about the way her sister would react.

Rational Therapy

Now let's look at a case presented by Ellis (1977), "The Treatment of a Psychopath with Rational Psychotherapy." Ellis describes this patient as follows:

The patient was a 25-year-old son of a well-to-do family and had been engaging in antisocial behavior, including lying, stealing, sexual irresponsibility, and physical assaults on others since the age of 14. He had been in trouble with the law on five different occasions, but had only been convicted once and spent one year in a reformatory. He displayed no guilt about his offenses and seemed not at all concerned about the fact that he had once helped cripple an old man whose candy store he and his youthful comrades had held up. He had two illegitimate children by different girls, but made no effort to see them or contribute to their financial support. He came for psychotherapy only at the insistence of his lawyer, who told him that his one chance of being put on probation, instead of being sent to prison, for his latest offense (rifling several vending machines) was for him to plead emotional disturbance and convince the court that he was really trying to do something to help himself in regard to this disturbance. (p. 261)

Ellis, after illustrating the way he attacked the patient's irrational thinking, then summarizes the treatment:

> . . . the therapist, in session after session with this intelligent psychopath, kept directly bringing up, ruthlessly examining, and forthrightly attacking some of his basic philosophies of living, and showing him that these philosophies underlay his antisocial thoughts and behavior. No criticism of or attack on the patient *himself* was made, but merely on his ideas, his thoughts, his assumptions which (consciously and unconsciously) served as the foundation stones for his disordered feelings and actions.
>
> After 22 sessions of this type of rational therapy, the patient finally was able to admit that for quite a long time he had vaguely sensed the self-defeatism and wrongness of his criminal behavior, but that he had been unable to make any concerted attack on it largely because he was afraid that he *couldn't* change it—that a) he had no ability to control his antisocial tendencies; and b) he felt that he would not be able to get along satisfactorily in life if he attempted to live more honestly. The therapist then started to make a frontal assault on the philosophies behind these defeatist feelings of the patient. He showed Jim that an individual's inability to control his behavior mainly stems from

the *idea* that he cannot do so—that long-standing feelings are innate and unmanageable and that one simply *has* to be ruled by them. Instead, the therapist insisted, human feelings *are* invariably controllable—if one seeks out the self-propagandizing sentences (e.g., "I must do this," "I have no power to stop myself from doing this," etc.) which one unconsciously uses to create and maintain these "feelings."

Jim's severe feelings of inadequacy—his original feelings that he never could gain the attention of others unless he was a problem child and his later feelings that he could not compete in a civilized economy unless he resorted to lying or thieving behavior—were also traced to the self-propagated beliefs behind them. . . . These self-sabotaging beliefs, and the internalized sentences continually maintaining them, were then not merely traced to their source (in Jim's early relations with his parents, teachers, and peers) but were logically analyzed, questioned, challenged, and counter-attacked by the therapist, until Jim learned to do a similar kind of self-analyzing, questioning, and challenging himself. (pp. 264–5)

Therapy lasted a total of 31 sessions, and a follow-up two years later indicated that Jim had turned into a "forward-looking citizen."

By using rational therapy, Ellis was able to uncover the trauma (not clearly specified, but involving Jim's early relations with his parents, teachers, and peers). This led Jim to believe that he could only get attention by being a problem child, and so he became a problem child, and then some, to avoid the bad feelings that came from not getting attention. By attacking his belief systems, Ellis was able to help him understand that the danger he feared, not getting attention, was avoidable, and that there were better ways to get that attention.

I admire the outcome that Ellis had with his patient. I doubt that I could have been successful with him, and even doubt that I could have kept him in therapy, although the alternative of going to prison would have helped with the latter goal. In my clinic, we don't attempt to do therapy with patients who are not motivated to change; if they're coming to see us merely because someone else wants them to, we usually ask them to return when *they* have a wish to see us. I fully understand that some of them may indeed wish to see us but just can't admit it. Nonetheless, if cooperation cannot be elicited in the first few sessions, we generally terminate "treatment" until the motivation is stronger. This does not apply to children or teenagers.

A Similar But Much Milder Case

This patient was a tall, nervous, very intense woman in her late thirties who sounded as though a great deal of anger was being barely contained through great effort. She said that she had come for therapy because she acted in ways that she didn't wish to act. She was specifically distressed by the rage she displayed toward her pets, the undue anger she vented on her husband, and the shoplifting that she did at a store in which she worked.

I learned that she was the youngest of four children from a close-knit family. By the time she had reached the eighth grade her older siblings had already left home and she was allowed to do anything that she pleased. Because her siblings had gotten into many episodes of what she described as "social difficulties," she had tried extra hard to please her parents.

It sounded as though, when she went off to college, there was a split in her personality between the side that could do anything it pleased and the side that wanted to please her parents. This was manifest on one hand by going to wild parties and being very promiscuous, and on the other by being a leader in a crusading religious organization, being an outstanding student, being appointed to committees by the dean, etc. She still felt this split, which had tormented her for years.

Obtaining that history, explaining ego state therapy to her, and introducing her to hypnosis occupied the first session.

On the second visit we learned through ego state therapy that when she was eleven she had cheated to beat one of her sisters at a childhood game and had thoroughly enjoyed the thrill of victory. Since then she had lied, cheated, stolen, etc., to gain good things for herself.

The "part" that caused this behavior was able to acknowledge that she now had the competence to obtain many good things for herself in better ways and that in doing so she would gain more self-respect and more respect from others simultaneously.

When she came out of the hypnosis, she said that she felt much better and had the feeling that she could control things now. We agreed that she would contact me again if need be. We terminated after that second session.

Ten months later she returned, saying that she had to talk about the difficulty she was having in dealing with her husband's autoerotic practices. None of her former difficulties had returned.

A More Severe Personality Disorder; Symptom Analysis with Hypnotic Techniques

This case was referred to me by another therapist in our clinic who knew that I was interested in working with personality disorders. She had interviewed this man and felt that his problems were too deep-seated and pervasive to be treated within the 20-visit limitation of our clinic.

He was a 39-year-old homosexual who initially expressed a variety of complaints. He had frequent bouts of depression and a painful lack of self-esteem, he described himself as a pathological liar, he repetitively sabotaged good jobs and consequently was often out of work and financially troubled, and he acceded to his mother's outrageous demands at great cost to himself.

Inquiry revealed that his depressions were brief, one to three days in duration, and always related to specific disappointments in his life. He attributed his low self-esteem to the fact that his family had always berated him, and we were able to consolidate his other complaints into one symptom—self-destructive behavior. His homosexuality did not seem to him to be a problem, so I did not choose to make it an issue in therapy. His primary concern was learning to control his self-destructive behavior, so that became our first target symptom.

In session two he was introduced to hypnosis and the corridor of time was used. This brought him back to age ten, and he saw himself cowering in a corner as his mother and father were fighting physically and verbally with one another. His father yelled at him that he was a bastard, denied paternity, and made other terrible insulting commentaries. He felt terribly hurt, as one might expect.

I suggested that perhaps he was afraid that if he developed close relationships with others they might hurt him as his father had. He confirmed this. (It's possible that I simply "inquired" if this were true. Either way, it's actually a suggestion, as any interpretation is bound to be.)

Next, I pointed out that, although his lying and his sabotaging jobs drove others away and protected him from the danger of their hurting him, that type of behavior caused numerous other problems and was probably no longer necessary: His father was out of the picture now, and most people are not nearly as cruel as his father was; he is now a grown man, not a frightened ten-year-old, and has better ways of protecting himself if others should become insulting; and driving away potential friends deprives him of the help that friends can offer in dealing with the many problems of day-to-day living. He agreed that he could now protect himself by being selective in choosing his friends and by rejecting them more honestly if he decided to do that.

At session three he declared that there had been a noticeable decrease in lying. He still did it occasionally but became aware of it very quickly, apologized to the other person immediately, and then told the truth. (I know he had been a pathological liar, and this report of early significant improvement could be just another example of that pathology; still, I believed him.)

Since there was early evidence of improvement in his self-destructive behavior, we then turned to the issue of his low self-esteem. Again, using ego state therapy, we learned that the highly critical part of his personality developed at age three, when his sister was born. He felt that from that time onward his parents "pushed him aside," ignored him, and criticized everything he did. As in the earlier cases I described of patients with low self-esteem, his self-criticism was designed to help him strive to be better by making him feel that he was currently not good enough. I used essentially the same advice about using kindly, constructive criticism instead of being so harsh with himself.

At session four he reported that his lying was under excellent control now and that he was feeling better about himself than he ever remembered feeling. He spent most of the session elaborating on those themes.

Session five was two weeks later. He said that he was doing very nicely, was recontacting old friends whom he had driven away by his lying and was getting along well with them now. He said that he felt very good but had some vague discomfort, as though he no longer knew himself. I responded that I wasn't certain what that meant, but perhaps it was due to his feeling and acting so differently that he was unfamiliar with himself in this new role; soon he'd feel at home with it. By the next visit that complaint was gone.

When he was next seen again, one month later, the above gains had been maintained. Now he told me that he had felt guilty about having sex ever since his sister had found him experimenting with a female cousin when he was nine. She had blackmailed him by threatening to tell his mother about it, and he had been so frightened of his mother's anger that he had let his sister get away with this until he was 25. Although this childhood incident sounded as though it might well be the source of his guilt, we agreed to search for any other possible causes at our next session.

In session seven the corridor of time was used. This took him back to the age of seven and a scene in which his mother had caught him in some sexual play with older boys. She had punished him harshly, verbally and physically. With this new information in hand, I speculated that allowing his sister to blackmail him so long was a symptom designed to protect him from another painful episode of his mother's punishment. His current guilt about sex could be seen as another, but ineffective, symptom designed to protect him in the same way. That is, if he felt guilty enough not to engage in sex, he could avoid his mother's punishment.

He was able to understand very quickly that this old danger was no longer applicable, and at the next session, his eighth, he gave some glowing reports of his progress. He was enjoying a new job and was doing well at it. He was handling the day-to-day problems of life better than he had in the past. Although he had had no sex since the last visit, he had the feeling that the guilt was gone.

Six weeks later he returned for session nine, reporting that he had been sexually active and had had no guilt about it. He was still doing well on his job and was still having good relations with his friends. He was not lying anymore, had stopped acceding to his mother's unreasonable demands, and was feeling quite good about himself.

He was last seen almost four months later and called me several months after that. The visit and the call were both about unrelated incidents, and all the previous gains were still being maintained.

Discussion

Although this patient and the previous one were both different from the psychopath treated with rational therapy, they serve to illustrate that even long-standing personality disorders can be managed in brief therapy, sometimes, by using symptom analysis.

In dealing with these individuals, however, I believe it best not to think of them as having personality disorders. That diagnosis carries such a dreary prognosis that it discourages many therapists. The classical theories for the origin and treatment of these disorders are so complex that if they are believed they lead to long and arduous therapies.

Instead, one might deal with personality disorders better by looking at the *symptoms* as the patient presents them and not worrying too much about the *traits* as described in *DSM-III-R*. As the symptoms are analyzed and relieved one by one, many of the traits disappear, and before too long it would be difficult to diagnose the patient as having a personality disorder.

I've had little success with some of the personality disorders. I've never been successful with a paranoid personality disorder. I've begun to think of this pathology as being primarily a thought disorder, and I suspect that the paranoid, like the other patients with primary thought disorders, may have too strong a biological component for cure through symptom analysis.

My successes with avoidant personality disorders have paled in comparison to their successes in avoiding any serious therapeutic engagement with me. Severe borderlines have not done well with me, although milder cases have done very well. One such case was described in some detail in my earlier book (Edelstien, 1981).

Having described the principles and practice of symptom analysis, I'll point out what must be obvious to some readers: although this is basically an insight-oriented therapy, transference and resistance were scarcely touched upon, at least in the traditional sense. Psychoanalysis, the forerunner of all the insight-oriented therapies, uses transference and resistance as its main cornerstones. Surprisingly, I, too, believe that transference is a cornerstone of the therapy that I do, but my perspective is hardly classical and thus requires some elaboration. Let's look at that perspective next.

7 | TRANSFERENCE AND RESISTANCE

TRANSFERENCE IS traditionally regarded as the inappropriate experiencing of feelings, attitudes, defenses, etc., toward some person in the present when those reactions actually are displaced from significant persons of early childhood.

What we have is a *process* of displacing, or transferring feelings, and an arbitrary limitation on the period from which this transfer may occur (early childhood), from whom it may occur (significant persons), and to whom it may be transferred (some person in the present). For discussion's sake, let's look at what happens if we remove those arbitrary limitations.

First, let's remove the limitation of transferring feelings from one person to another. This would permit us to include places, situations, and objects. Next, let's remove the limitation of time, so the transference need not come from early childhood. With this expanded definition of transference, then, look at what we have:

If a young child were bitten by a large dog, and as an adult continued to have a fear of large dogs, that would be a transference reaction. If an adolescent girl were sexually molested by a family member, and as a consequence could feel only repulsion when, as an adult, she had sex with her husband, that would be a transference reaction. If an adult with panic disorder had an episode in a restaurant and then was afraid to enter any restaurant, that would be a transference reaction.

In the introduction I suggested that the development of a transference reaction was not necessary for effective therapy. With this expanded definition of transference, it's easy to see that patients come to their first session with all the transference they need—and with all the transference that we need to help them.

We can assume that their symptoms are defensive maneuvers intended to protect them from experiencing again the bad feelings that resulted from some traumatic experience. We can assume that they are transferring to other persons, places, or things the emotional responses that they had to the source of that trauma, and that they are transferring their old defensive maneuvers as well. From this perspective, then, *the analysis of a symptom is actually the analysis of a transference reaction*. No other transference reactions need be analyzed to give the patient good and long lasting benefits.

It should be noted that, even though I would be inclined to call the symptom a transference reaction, others will have other names. The analyst probably would not accept my expanded definition and would call the symptom merely a symptom. The behaviorist might call it a conditioned response. The rational or cognitive therapist might call it the result of a self-propagated belief, and so forth.

Transferences are typically classified as positive or negative when the restricted definition is used. This same classification would be applicable to the expanded definition; e.g., if a young child had a gentle, loving dog as a pet and thereafter had a fondness for dogs, this could be classified as a positive transference. The hypothetical child mentioned a few paragraphs ago would have a negative transference.

Transferences could also be classified another way: those that are deliberately encouraged by the therapist and those that are not. The short-term therapist would rarely encourage the development of a transference because that, along with its ensuing resolution, would lead to long-term therapy. The long-term therapist usually does encourage its development, believing that the feelings transferred to *the therapist* are beneficial in understanding and resolving the patient's problems. Using our expanded definition of a transference, this may not be necessary.

But transferences develop to the therapist, whether the therapist encourages them or not. I have nothing new to say about their management when they occur. Presumably each therapist has already learned techniques for dealing with transference. However, I do have an observation to make.

In my patients, the transferences that are so strongly positive that they interfere with therapy are far fewer now than they were ten years ago, when my hair was thicker and my waist was not. Probably my hair and waist have little to do with that.

What probably has more to do with it is the fact that now I see patients more briefly and keep them so busily focused on their symptoms, their strengths, and their own abilities to solve their problems that there is little time, at least in the office, for them to develop fantasies about me. In my cases presented in Chapter 6, only once did a transference reaction make itself apparent, and that was toward the hypnotic process, not toward me. It was resolved by a few minutes of our discussing the patient's prior experience with hypnosis.

Resistance

Rarely is it necessary to analyze resistance when one works with short-term techniques. In our case illustrations resistance appeared only twice. Once was with the patient who had the transference resistance mentioned above; the second was with the patient who at one session would only nod her head instead of speak. This resistance had dissipated by the next session without any specific attempts on my part to analyze it.

There are instances, however, in which resistance is considerably more of a problem. Before looking at a method for dealing with these resistances by symptom analysis, let's first look at resistances in general.

Resistances may occur at any stage of therapy; they may even prevent a patient from entering therapy. Conversely, there may be resistance to ending therapy. In between, the patient may miss sessions, come late, terminate early, or avoid revealing needed information. S/he may do the latter by being silent or by talking excessively about unrelated matters. The withheld information may be historical data or the expression of feelings. The patient may also display resistance by showing no change despite having given copious information and obtaining an understanding of it.

Resistances may be conscious or not. They may be rational or not. The patient may consciously withhold information and do so quite rationally if s/he has one of those therapists who makes each interpretation into an insulting commentary about the patient, his/her actions, or his/her feelings. Unfortunately, this happens more often than we'd like to believe. The patient will also resist making changes, if s/he believes, consciously or not, that the changes would be dangerous.

A resistance is any maneuver that the patient makes that interferes with the progress of therapy. Since we believe therapy to be a process that will enhance the patient's life, we can then say that a resistance is a behavior that interferes with his/her life. Isn't this precisely what a symptom is?

When we look at resistances, we can also see that they serve precisely the same function as any other symptom, i.e., they protect the patient from experiencing some bad feelings again, or conversely, they may help him/her achieve some reward. Like other symptoms, they generally arise from prior experiences. A few hypothetical examples might illustrate this: "I felt humiliated when I let my feelings come pouring out and resolved I'd never do that again." "I felt ashamed when my therapist pointed out that I hated my mother, and didn't want him to know how I really felt about my father." "He wanted me to start going to supermarkets again, but I had a panic attack in one once, and I'm not going to do it." "If my problems go away, I'll have to return to work." The patient may or may not be consciously aware of these sentiments.

If we see resistances as nothing more than symptoms related to therapy, symptom analysis can be used just as it would be for any other symptom. Fortunately, resistances are uncommon in my patients, so there are only a couple of cases to offer for illustration. One is relatively new, while the other has been reported before (Edelstien, 1982). Both involve resistance to change.

Case Illustration #1

This patient was a graduate student who had entered therapy because of a number of mild obsessive-compulsive type complaints, as well as her inability to enjoy sex with her husband. The latter was really an obsessive-compulsive type complaint, too, because the main issue seemed to be her fear of loss of control if she had an orgasm. We had worked together six or eight sessions, and although she had given me a good quantity of information about early traumas that seemed like probable sources of her various difficulties, and although I had attempted the type of maneuvers described earlier, no change was occurring.

We discussed her resistance and decided to try ego state therapy to learn about that part of her that was preventing change from occurring. This technique brought her back to a traumatic event in which she was a young child and her father was very angry with her.

Exploration of this event revealed that her father had often fussed at her because she didn't eat enough. One evening, in order to please her father, she had put a very large quantity of spaghetti on her plate. He became very angry, yelling at her that she had taken so much spaghetti that now there wasn't enough for the rest of the family. He didn't talk to her again for several days.

I asked if this had made her afraid of changing old patterns of behavior, and she replied that it had. I then pointed out the many behavior changes that she had undergone as she had grown up (learning to read, do math, ride a bike, drive a car, etc.), and how people had been pleased, not angry, because of those. I pointed out the specific changes she had said she wanted to make through therapy and helped the ego state see that these would be appreciated by the people who were now in her life. In view of this, I wondered, would the ego state now be willing to let her change?

The ego state was a little reluctant, saying that she had been doing things the old way for a long time and wasn't sure what would happen if she changed. I asked, would she be willing to change slowly, and thus be able to see, bit by bit, if it were truly safe? She agreed to that proposition, and from that time on changes started occurring, but slowly.

Case Illustration #2

This was a 65-year-old man who had recently retired and who had married for the first time only five years earlier. He had been in therapy with a number of therapists on a number of occasions (including sessions with me about ten years earlier), but had received little or no benefit.

He had spent a lifetime trying, successfully, to be as unobtrusive as possible. He had always felt dominated by his older brother. Although he had a number of issues he wanted to discuss, perhaps the one that bothered him the most was that he found he could not take time now to do things just for himself. For years he had looked forward to retiring and finally having the time to do a number of things he had always wanted to do but could never get around to because of his obsessive need to attend to all of his "duties."

Using hypnotic techniques previously described, we were able to uncover seemingly significant explanations for his symptoms, but little change occurred. He did become slightly more assertive, but he still could not spend time doing things just for himself. We used ego state therapy along the same lines mentioned in the previous case, trying to learn about the part of his personality that was preventing change from occurring.

We uncovered a series of traumas from his childhood, in each of which he had been humiliated, or simply angered, because his parents would never let him enjoy any accomplishment unless he shared it with his older brother. Thus, if he auditioned and was accepted into the cast of a school play, he could not participate unless his brother could also be in the play. If he were elected to an organization, he couldn't join unless his brother could also join. There were a number of such incidents, so he had finally decided to stop doing things "just for himself."

The ego state was able to understand that the situation was different now. His brother lived in a different state, his parents were deceased and could no longer hold sway over him, and he would no longer have to suffer the same humiliations if he did things well just for himself. The "part" agreed to let him try again.

I wish that I could say we had fantastic results after this session. We did not, but a year after our last session, which was only one or two sessions after dealing with the resistance, telephone contact revealed that he was now in an art class, which was something that he could not have joined before; he was enjoying it and was planning to do more painting. His level of assertiveness would hardly be mistaken for Rambo's, but it sounded as though his in-laws and his brother were no longer the sources of intense troubles they had been; this was due, in part, to his refusal to let them treat him as they had in the past.

I was disappointed that I could not have been of more help to this nice man, but that is not the issue here. The issue is that analyzing a resistance in this manner enabled us to overcome it, at least in part, and that some change was able to occur where none had occurred previously. Perhaps even that much change in a 65-year-old patient with obsessive-compulsive traits should be appreciated.

Symptom analysis with hypnotic techniques is my preferred way of dealing with resistances, at least in those patient with whom an insight-oriented therapy is being used, but obviously there are a great number of other methods. Traditionally, therapists may use their own silence to overcome a patient's resistance when it is being manifested by silence; the patient's increasing anxiety about the prolonged silence stimulates him/her to speak again. Although traditional therapists may not like to view it this way, one could say that they are using a behavior therapy technique, negative reinforcement (punishment) for not speaking.

At times the therapist may merely point out the patient's maneuvers of resistance and they will cease. Analyzing the resistance, though, is the main means of dealing with it. No matter what techniques of analysis are used, it is highly probable that the analyst will find that the resistance was an attempt to protect the patient from some real or imaginary danger, just as we find with the analysis of other symptoms.

O'Hanlon (1987) has listed some of the ways in which Milton Erickson dealt with resistances. Sometimes he would do these things with hypnosis, but often without. A few of his techniques were: prescribing a resistance, giving the illusion of alternatives, and using indirect rather than direct suggestions.

Basically the idea behind prescribing a resistance is that the only way a patient can resist the prescription is by complying with whatever the therapist had wished originally, and if he accepts the prescription, he is complying by doing so. This is what many of us did instinctively when our three-year-old children were being negativistic, and I personally find it difficult to treat a patient the same way.

An example of giving the illusion of alternatives is to tell the patient, "You can do . . . now, or you can do it tomorrow." When I tried this, my patients usually did neither. I thought, "Maybe 'tomorrow' is too definite a time, so let's change it to 'later'." I changed it, but then, if my patients followed the suggestion, it was usually so much later that I never knew about it.

Using indirect suggestions makes the patient less resistant because s/he's not fully aware that something is being suggested. In my limited experience of trying to use indirect suggestions, my patients have been so totally unaware that something was being suggested that they hardly ever followed the suggestions—thus my limited experience.

My own failures with these Ericksonian methods should not be viewed as a criticism of the methods, for they apparently work well for other therapists. This does serve as an illustration, though, of why it is probably best to alter techniques not only according to the needs of the patient but also according to the abilities of the therapist. My own abilities are compatible with the techniques that I described above, and I hope that they will work well for some of you, too.

III | *PSYCHOLOGICAL DISORDERS WITH OBVIOUS ORIGINS*

8 | NONINSIGHT-ORIENTED THERAPY

THERE ARE MANY therapists who never use insight-oriented therapy for any of their work, relying instead on behavior therapy, cognitive therapy, strategic therapy, etc. For those therapists who do choose to use insight-oriented therapy and who have a fondness for helping patients understand the origins of their problems, there are still many cases in which this type of work is not indicated.

Insight-oriented therapy usually is not attempted with those patients who are judged to lack the capacity to do insight-oriented work, although I suspect more patients are categorized this way than should be. The prevalent attitude is stated by Werman (1984, p. 13), "In contrast, supportive psychotherapy assumes that the patient's psychological equipment is fundamentally inadequate."

Using hypnotic techniques described in the previous section, I've seen patients who might be poor candidates for traditional insight-oriented therapy successfully engage in what I'd consider insight-oriented therapy, although I'd call it symptom analysis. Werman himself, in the rest of his book, displays much more flexibility than the quoted statement would indicate. He even acknowledges that some insight is often gained during supportive therapy.

For me, that raises a number of questions: Is it really true that these patients' psychological equipment is "fundamentally inadequate"? Are our assumptions about this too often erroneous? Shouldn't we consider that it's really our techniques that are "fundamentally inadequate"? Like most questions, these are more easily asked than answered, and I shall not attempt the latter.

Other groups of patients for whom insight is not sought are those for whom the origins of the problems are so readily apparent that insight is not necessary, and those for whom the problems are primarily biological. For the last group the insight will come from the probings of the geneticists and the psychobiologists, not from the traditional therapist.

One group of cases in which the psychological cause is readily apparent would be the simple phobias of recent origin. Examples would be: "Since my automobile accident, I'm terrified of getting in a car again", or "I had my first panic attack while I was in a restaurant. Ever since then I'm unable to go to restaurants and I start shaking and sweating if I even think about doing so," or perhaps, the case of a young boy by the name of Hans who gets frightened by a falling horse and develops a phobia of horses after that incident.

Other cases in which the psychological origins would be clear would include the post-traumatic stress syndromes, acute, chronic, or delayed. There are interesting similarities between the simple phobias and the post-traumatic stress syndromes: Both are anxiety responses to frightening incidents; both may occur immediately following the incidents or many years after, often with no apparent precipitant; both occur in some people but not all people who experienced the same trauma.

Although the phobias are not classified into subdivisions in the same manner as the post-traumatic stress syndromes, (PTSS) are, I believe that they could be, and probably should be, because that would give more direction to the types of therapy that might be employed. In this classification there would be the acute phobias, such as the examples recently cited. There would be the chronic ones, which, like chronic PTSS, had existed for six months or more after the trauma. Both of these would be included in psychological disorders with obvious origins, so insight therapy would not be needed.

Then, analogous to delayed PTSS, there would be the delayed phobias, i.e., those that first appeared long after the original trauma. Since the memories of the original trauma usually would have been repressed, insight-oriented therapy could prove to be useful, although not necessary.

Differences between a phobia and a PTSS include: the intensity of the symptoms, the greater difficulty in treating the PTSS, and often, the intensity of the trauma involved. The last difference is not consistent, for the same trauma, say an industrial accident, may cause minimal post-traumatic anxiety in one patient, a phobic reaction in a second, and a full-blown PTSS in a third.

For example, if the night clerk in a convenience store were robbed at gun point, beaten, and threatened with death, and then he came to a therapist saying, "I know that there are security guards now and that I've been assigned to daytime duty so that there's really no danger, but every time I even think about returning to that store I get so frightened I just can't go," he would be diagnosed as having a simple phobia, and most therapists would attribute it to his recent harrowing experience. If, following exactly the same incident, he came to a therapist and said, "I keep having vivid images of the gunman. When I finally drift off to sleep at 2 or 3 o'clock in the morning I have terrifying nightmares about men shooting at me. I jump and start sweating anytime I hear a loud noise. I can't concentrate on anything. I'm not interested in going out and doing things or in seeing my old friends," then he would be diagnosed as having an acute post-traumatic stress syndrome.

If that patient came into a therapist's office, I would hope that most therapists would assume that the ordeal mentioned above was the origin of his difficulties. However, those therapists who adhere too closely to the formulation that Langs espouses would be forced to assume that the robbery was almost incidental, that the real basis of the symptoms lay in unresolved infantile fantasies and drives which had been reawakened by the trauma. They would believe that the patient could receive no lasting benefits until those infantile problems had been resolved. As a consequence of that line of thinking, it is quite possible that it would be a very, very long time before the patient received any benefits at all.

There may be some slight justification for this Langsian position. It is known that not all people who go through this type of trauma will suffer so severely from it that professional help will be needed. Those who do respond so strongly, therefore, must be different from those who don't. One might claim, then, that the difference is in how infantile drives and wishes were resolved earlier. One might claim this, but no one can prove it, so other explanations are entitled to equal consideration: Catecholamine metabolism, other, nonspecific genetic endowments, or concurrent life stresses are among the possibilities. It is probable that more than one of these possibilities coexist.

Phobias that have appeared shortly after some easily recognizable trauma are most commonly treated with a desensitization technique. Either progressive desensitization or "flooding" may be used. The former is gentler; the latter, quicker. Indirect suggestion, one of the many hypnotic techniques of Milton Erickson, may also be used by those therapists who have learned how to do that work.

My own preference is to use hypnosis for "flooding" the patient. By this I mean having the patient go into hypnosis, have a vivid image of being at the scene of the trauma, letting him/her endure the painful emotions, and helping him/her understand that nothing bad is happening. Additionally, I generally help him/her visualize a strongly positive outcome to the event. Not infrequently, one session of this type of work eliminates the phobia.

A Simple Phobia Caused by a Panic Attack

A 36-year-old woman with panic disorder developed a driving phobia after having a panic attack while driving. Not only was she unable to drive, but she was also unable to ride as a passenger in the car; consequently, her activities had become badly restricted. She felt sad and guilty about this because her family's activities had also become restricted as a result of her illness. Even though the panic disorder had been well controlled with the use of an antidepressant medication, the phobia persisted.

She was hypnotized and told to imagine herself in the back seat of her car while it was still parked in the driveway. She followed this suggestion and displayed a mild degree of anxiety in doing so. I then suggested that the car doors were locked and she was unable to exit. More anxiety was evident from her increased respiratory rate and the tightening of her skeletal muscles. The next suggestions were that her teenaged daughter had entered the driver's seat, had started the engine, a glass partition had separated the back and front seats, and her daughter could not hear her and did not know that she was in the back.

I then took her on an imaginary trip, further and further from home, entering a crowded freeway with cars speeding along on both sides. Her anxiety increased as the story unfolded. After a short while I suggested that even though she was feeling highly anxious, she was beginning to become aware that nothing bad was happening. Her anxiety continued, but now it began to subside slightly.

As she continued on this trip, I made repeated comments that she was becoming more and more aware that nothing bad was happening. She became more relaxed. Soon, I was suggesting that now she was beginning to enjoy the trip and the beautiful scenery that she was passing (described in some detail). Next, she was feeling the freedom that came from being mobile once again, and as the glass partition came down, she had the pleasure of visiting with her daughter as they drove along.

By this time there were no visible signs of anxiety. I added a few more frills and then had her imagine herself at home again, very pleased with herself for being able to be in a car and having nothing bad happen.

That was the only session devoted to the phobia. About a month later she called me, thrilled that she had been able to go on a trip to Tahoe with her family. It was only after they had been in the car for several hours that she became aware of her accomplishment. She had been so busy enjoying the scenery and the outing with her family that she had forgotten about having a phobia.

I must add that this technique doesn't always work this quickly or this well. Often it does, however, and I believe that it's well worth trying for any similar case. When it hasn't worked, I've tried searching for earlier antecedents to explain the phobia, and occasionally I've found them, with resultant success, but that doesn't work all the time, either.

The flooding technique of desensitization could have been done without hypnosis. The patient could have been locked in the car and driven around until her fear subsided. There are some who might find that the use of hypnosis is easier on the patient and the therapist. Progressive desensitization could have been used instead by assigning the patient the task of gradually exposing herself to longer and longer journeys in the car. But flooding is faster.

A Post-Traumatic Stress Disorder

Although some PTSS are exceedingly difficult to treat, there are others that respond very well to the same desensitizing techniques used for the phobias.

This patient was a woman in her mid-twenties who had been assaulted at home one night. She had stepped out of her shower and found an intruder in her apartment. He beat her, bound her, and then proceeded to rummage through her belongings, taking those that he wanted. This event had occurred about a year before she came to see me.

She presented as depressed, withdrawn from her social contacts and from her usual activities. She had a startle reflex, had recurrent nightmares about the assault, was frightened to be alone at home, could not sleep without the lights on, and was unable to function well enough to hold a job.

Under hypnosis she followed my suggestions that she go through the event again but without the physical pain. She appeared terrified as she did so. After a brief (30-second) exposure to this trauma, she was instructed to let the images fade, relax, rest, and realize that she was safe once again. Then, with her permission, I had her repeat the process, after first telling her that this time the feelings would not be as strong.

We repeated this several times, always with the suggestion that the feelings would be less intense than they had been the time before. After several run-throughs, there were virtually no external signs of discomfort. Next, I had her go through the scene a final time, emerging from it with a feeling of mastery. Although it had been an extremely dangerous situation, she had had the intelligence, the courage, the luck, or some other resource that had enabled her to come out of it basically intact. She was a survivor! Whatever resources she had used to survive were still hers and available for to use in other situations. She would now feel righteous rage at what had happened, but no longer would she let her assailant have any further control over her life or her feelings.

Her response was not as dramatic as in the case of the woman with the driving phobia, but within two weeks she was clearly better, and within six weeks she was essentially back to her premorbid condition.

In these cases it's easily seen that the basic principles of symptom analysis still apply, although no uncovering work was required. In each instance the patient quickly presented information about the origin of the traumatic event and the feelings evoked. In the phobias it was easy to see that avoidance was being used to prevent a recurrence of the painful feelings. In the case of the woman who had been assaulted and who had developed a PTSS, not all of the symptoms can be seen as protective, and I would tend to classify them as painful feelings that were still being evoked by the trauma. The actual therapeutic steps involved helping the patients fully understand that the old dangers were now gone.

9 | ADJUSTMENT DISORDERS

A THIRD GROUP OF CASES in which insight is not needed are those we call "adjustment disorders." I'll start with a hypothetical example: A high school senior comes into the office complaining that his girlfriend just left him and he is depressed, and is sleeping poorly. His condition would be diagnosed as an adjustment disorder. Most clinicians would assume that the girlfriend's departure was the source of his trouble and would proceed to treat him accordingly. He would probably recover in short order. Other clinicians, believing that they had to analyze earlier events, would start on a search for early object losses, and the young man would be in therapy for a long, long time.

Before going further, let's look closely at the category, "adjustment disorder," for we can see an interesting possibility: This disorder may represent the initial phase through which patients go prior to developing more complex disorders. (Here I'm excluding those diagnoses that have a primarily biological origin.)

From this longer-range perspective, the anxiety, depression, etc., that are displayed initially and which are commonly called the symptoms of the adjustment disorder would not be considered symptoms per se, but would be seen as the painful feelings that follow any traumatic incident. Later, if the patient adopted inappropriate behaviors to protect himself from experiencing those feelings again, we would call those new behaviors the symptoms of a phobia, sexual dysfunction, personality disorder, etc. Earlier case examples illustrated how this could occur; perhaps a hypothetical scenario will aid the illustration.

If we use the fictitious young man mentioned above as an example, and if we remember the trauma theory's explanation of how psychiatric problems develop, we see that (1) this young man had a traumatic experience, (2) he had painful feelings as a result of this experience (the "symptoms" of the adjustment disorder), and (3) he is now in a position either to resolve the problem in a healthy manner or, unfortunately, to find inappropriate ways to protect himself from these bad feelings in the future. The latter course, I believe, is what leads him into some other diagnostic category.

If he resolves the problem on his own, as most such young men do, his instinctive methods for doing so may well bear a remarkable similarity to some of those formal therapeutic techniques that do not utilize insight.

He may wallow in his misery, exposing himself to the full intensity of it for some short while until it passes, or he may start dating other girls immediately, exposing himself to all of the fears that he has about doing so. In either case, this is like the "flooding" of behavior therapy.

He may, instead, start talking to girls only in groups or on the phone, seeing them only at parties, or going out only once or twice with any one girl rather than letting himself become more involved with a female friend. This is a very real progressive desensitization.

He may tell himself that if the girlfriend treated him in this fickle, callous way, he's lucky to have found out what she's really like before he became more deeply committed. He may tell himself that the fact that she rejected him doesn't mean that all women will do so, and having attracted her is evidence that he has the ability to attract other women, too. Here we have the essential ingredients of cognitive therapy.

He may decide that he's not ready to date again yet, but that this is a good time to engage in other activities. He may start going around more with his buddies to build up a better social network. He may start an exercise program to make himself more physically attractive. He may start a reading program to become more intellectually attractive, etc. Here we have the elements of strategic therapy.

There's also the possibility that there may be a little "insight". "Boy, I can see now that I acted like a nerd with her, and if I don't want to get hurt like this again, I'd better clean up my act."

On the other hand, if one of these happy resolutions does not occur, he might protect himself in other ways. He might act primarily from his anger at being jilted and treat women with contempt and cruelty thereafter, hurting them before they have a chance to hurt him. Or he might develop an excessive suspiciousness and extreme jealousy as attempts to prevent the possibility of his being hurt again by a girlfriend who leaves him for someone else. Either of those resolutions would then entitle him to the diagnosis of a personality disorder. In movies I've seen, this is how the hero's personality disorder developed. *Casablanca* is the only specific example I can remember, but I have many vague memories of John Wayne, John Garfield, and other strong, silent types sitting in a bar, treating some beautiful woman coldly, and having her say, "Someone must have hurt you bad." In patients that I've seen, however, it developed at earlier ages. The pathological jealousy usually developed over sibling rivalries that occurred during childhood—not infancy—and the "hurt them before they hurt me" attitude also came from childhood hurts.

Our fictitious young man could respond primarily from his fear of being jilted again, phobically avoid future relationships, and be diagnosed as phobic. He could respond primarily from shame, develop sexual problems, and be classified as having a disorder of sexual functioning. With a little ingenuity he could find other inappropriate resolutions and earn other appropriate diagnoses.

After taking only the briefest of histories, the therapist who saw this patient during the phase called "adjustment disorder" would know the source of the trauma and the painful feelings that it evoked. There would not yet be a protective symptom that had developed fully, but there might be early, impulsive behavior that would represent initial attempts at self-protection. The patient might be driving fast and recklessly as one means of hiding his feelings, fighting with his younger brother to displace his anger at the girlfriend, or using drugs to numb his sorrow. The therapist's task would be to help him find better solutions, and the only "insight" needed would be to help him see how the impulsive behavior was dangerously self-destructive.

About a year ago, I saw a patient who presented an extremely clear example of how the trauma theory applies to cases of adjustment disorder. She came to her appointment with the "symptom": "I don't want to have sex with my husband." I said that, if she didn't want to have sex with her husband, I didn't understand why she was seeking therapy. "He wanted me to come." I told her that I didn't want to treat her to try to get her to do something that she didn't want to do just because her husband wanted her to do it. She looked visibly relieved.

She told me that she didn't want to have sex with him because, although he was very nice in many ways, he was mean and hurtful in other ways and she knew that, if she had sex with him, she'd start feeling closer to him again and would end up getting hurt, as had happened many times before.

I replied that it was obvious that her "symptom" was a protection against getting hurt again, but that it wasn't the only way to avoid getting hurt. She should tell him exactly why she was afraid of having sex and let him know what changes would be necessary for her to feel safe again. If he were truly able to make those changes, not merely promise to make them, then sex would be safe; if not, then the old dangers remained. She left the office very pleased, saying that she would return depending on how things went after her discussion with him.

I do not know if the case is concluded. If the husband changes and she's able to have sex comfortably, it is. If the husband refuses to change or is unable to do so, it still may be concluded, or perhaps she'll wish to discuss how to stay in a sexless marriage. (She's presently content to do without sex.) If the husband changes but she's still unable to have sex comfortably, then I hope she returns so we can deal with that. It's been about a year, and she hasn't returned.

It might be argued that I could have helped her find another means of protecting herself: having sex without feeling more attached to him. I do not consider that a desirable option, but if she did, and if that's what she wanted, I don't know that I could help her achieve it. I simply wouldn't know how.

The symptoms of the adjustment disorder may be seen from a long-range perspective as the "painful feelings" which patients who later progress to a more complex diagnosis avoided by more remarkable symptomatic behavior. If we are fortunate enough to see patients during this earlier stage, we have the opportunity to help them find better solutions while the symptoms are still just painful feelings.

Of course, patients should be able to find the better solutions by themselves, and under less taxing situations they probably would. It seems to me, however, that patients who come to us for help in situations such as these do so because something is interfering with their normal coping skills. Among the interfering factors are: (1) feelings that are strong and painful, (2) confusion and indecision, and (3) wishful thinking. All of these interfering factors may be seen as attempts to ward off bad feelings of one type or another.

Strong and painful feelings almost always stimulate responses of one kind or another. Often these responses facilitate problem-solving, but when they're too intense they impede it. They may prompt precipitous, destructive behavior that worsens an already bad situation. They may cause withdrawal and immobility, making any constructive activity impossible. They may cloud judgment, disrupt communications, etc. If they're that severe, they must be reduced in intensity before any real progress can occur.

Constructive problem-solving cannot be expected if patients are confused about the source of the problem or about what solutions might be available. If they are too indecisive, no actions will be taken at all. If they avoid painful decisions that must be made because they're holding onto forlorn hopes that things will improve through the benevolence of others, they will never solve the problems themselves. If they avoid decision-making, others will often make decisions for them, and the results may not be so benevolent.

Since any of these impediments can significantly interfere with patients' abilities to solve problems, in the following chapters we will look at ways to remove them.

10 | REDUCING THE INTENSITY OF PAINFUL FEELINGS

THE INTENSITY OF THE painful feelings that are evoked by the traumatic situation does a great deal to deplete coping skills. Once the intensity of the feelings has been reduced, those skills become more available. There are both psychological and pharmacological methods for reducing that intensity.

Depressive Feelings

We know that when a patient is suffering from depression, usual patterns of eating and sleeping are altered. Physical energy is lacking. Mental abilities such as memory, concentration, problem-solving, and decision-making are impaired. Diminished ability to enjoy anything deprives the depressed person of the motivation to seek distracting pleasures. Increased irritability makes it more difficult to be around others, or for others to be around her/him. Excessive self-criticism makes the individual feel unworthy of deserving anything better than this sad lot and/or s/he doesn't believe s/he has the abilities to make things better. That is quite a burden to carry around while trying to find a better solution.

In cases where depression is prominent, an antidepressant medication often helps restore those lost abilities rather quickly. Among my cases, this seems to be true whether the depression is the result of some recent, known depressing event, on the one hand, or has no recognizable precipitant, on the other.

It's impossible to be certain that it's the antidepressant per se that initiates the beginning of improvement, for it may be that the mere contact with a "healer" started things moving in the right direction. It may even be that things had already begun an upward swing and that this produced the momentum to come for help. Still, it's my clinical impression that the patients who accept the prescriptions improve more quickly than those who don't. It's a firm impression, but only an impression. I have no concrete data with which to substantiate it. If my impression's correct, this proves nothing, because those who accept the prescription may be manifesting a greater faith in the powers of the healer, may be more inclined to believe that they deserve to get better, or may be displaying other psychological responses rather than mere biological ones. Whatever the reasons may be, since those who take the medication seem to feel better more quickly than those who don't, I offer it.

Many of the patients I've seen who entered therapy because they claimed they couldn't stand the stress of a job, school, a marriage, etc., have seemed to be clinically depressed. Antidepressant medicine would always be offered and usually accepted. Most of the time, within one or two weeks, sometimes even sooner, those patients would be eating and sleeping better, concentrating and thinking more clearly, feeling much less irritable, and getting along better with others. With those improvements, and often with no specific therapy related to external problem areas, the external problems were resolved and the patients no longer experienced difficulties at home, school, or on the job—or, more precisely, no difficulties severe enough to require outside intervention.

In those cases that did require outside intervention, this intervention became much more effective when patients had regained their emotional stability, their mental acuity, and their physical energy.

It's interesting to note the rapid improvement that many patients display, despite the fact that much literature says that antidepressant medications usually take two to three weeks to begin working. Having seen hundreds of patients who reported marked improvement in ten days, and many who said they were noticeably better in three or four, I have to question my diagnostic criteria, the validity of the patients' reports, the relevance of placebo effect, or the reliability of the literature.

I believe that I adhere to the *DSM-III-R* diagnostic criteria for depression, but I do not do rating scales before and after the institution of medication. The patient's voice, appearance, psychomotor activity, and reports of what is happening in his/her life lead me to conclude if improvement is evident or not. Additionally, although it is not a true rating scale, all of the patients who enter our clinic fill out a "Personal Data Sheet" (actually four sheets), which lists some 40 possible symptoms. The symptoms are checked off as "never," "rarely," "frequently," or "always." Asking about the symptoms after treatment has started, and finding that their frequency has been reduced, helps me judge about reported improvement.

There is probably a placebo effect in addition to the actual pharmacological one. When prescribing medication, I clearly announce my honest expectation that there may be significant improvement within a few days, and this may improve the patient's response. I don't think of that as being bad. As far as the literature is concerned, I have no reason to doubt it, other than the observation that many of my patients improve more rapidly than the literature would lead me to expect.

Improvement following the mere alleviation of the depressive symptoms has been such a common occurrence that I never consider "job burnout" as job burnout until we see how the patient is doing after being treated for depression. In the majority of cases, the job becomes tolerable again, and if there was ever any real enthusiasm for it, that enthusiasm often returns.

The same thing also occurs, but less frequently, in marriages that have become rocky and are near foundering. If one or both partners are depressed, we can be certain that they bring little joy to the marriage. They take no pleasure in any activities, are not interested in sex, may neglect their usual duties around the house, and are irritable and irritating. I've seen threatened marriages return to a solid foundation rather quickly with little more treatment than relieving the depression in the afflicted partner.

Of course, there are many other reasons why marriages fail, and I do not propose that this is the solution for all of them, or even the majority. In the significant number of cases in which it does work, however, we are able to see very clearly how patients become able to cope with their own problems when they're no longer overwhelmed by painful feelings.

Anxiety

Anxiety, we know, can produce many of the same disabling changes that depression produces. If the level of anxiety is so high that it interferes with the patient's normal functioning, an antianxiety medication can help the patient become a more constructive partner in the business of therapy. It may also help avert further difficulties. Whatever the distressing situation may be, I cannot conceive of its being made better by the patient's losing his job, doing poorly at school, or encountering some of the other complications that could occur from an inability to perform at his/her normal level. Additionally, I don't believe that either the patient or I benefit from struggling to find a better solution while s/he is unable to concentrate well, remember well, or think with usual clarity.

Because most of the antianxiety medications can become habit-forming rather easily, I hesitate using them for any extended period of time or using them at all unless the level of anxiety impedes the process of therapy or seems to be endangering aspects of the patients' lives. Simple relaxation exercises, including self-hypnosis, can be learned quickly and often suffice. The antidepressant medications, which are not habit-forming, will often help alleviate anxiety even in those patients who are not depressed.

Medication and relaxation techniques are not the only ways to relieve anxiety. If indeed therapy works primarily by helping the patient understand that a certain danger no longer exists or that there are better ways of defending oneself, then it seems logical first to see if the danger is still present.

As an example, a school teacher came to our clinic because his anxiety and depression had incapacitated him for about a month. His symptoms developed when his principal gave him an evaluation that was slightly below those he had received for many years. He spoke to her about it and she told him he shouldn't take it so seriously, adding, "I came down on you pretty hard."

Somehow, he had focused only on, "I came down on you pretty hard," interpreting this as meaning that she would continue to come down on him pretty hard. To him this meant that his career and livelihood were in jeopardy.

I merely explained that I thought he was misinterpreting what had occurred. She said he shouldn't take it too seriously; it sounded to me as though she was apologizing for coming down on him *too* hard. He thought about this briefly, recognized that as the most likely possibility, realized that the dangers he had been fearing were not present, calmed down quickly, and returned to his job soon thereafter.

Another teacher, whom I had treated previously for an entirely different problem, called for an appointment, saying that his father had recently died and he felt the need to talk with me.

When he came in for the appointment, he said that he was handling his grief okay, but there was something else he had to discuss. He had gone to the funeral of a friend. The minister conducted the ceremony in his customary manner and then dismissed the congregation without going through a particular ritual that should have been followed. Shortly after that, the patient's father-in-law died.

The patient went to that funeral, the minister again left out the same ritual, and soon thereafter the patient's father died. The patient was now afraid to go to church anymore, fearing that this could lead to the death of another family member. He was so concerned about this possibility that he had even spent considerable time thinking about who the next victim most likely would be.

A little cognitive therapy about drawing sweeping conclusions from inadequate evidence and discussion of post hoc reasoning had no effect, but when I asked, "Do you really believe that your God is so unfair and so vengeful that He'd kill a member of your family just because some minister made a mistake?" He thought briefly and said, "No, my God is a just God." He smiled with relief, and that one short session ended his problem. At another visit, four months later, for another problem, that intervention was still working.

In those cases in which the patient knows that the dangers are not real yet still reacts as though they were, I would generally try insight-oriented therapy, but for those cases in which the dangers actually do exist, the patient must be helped to develop better defensive techniques. As an example, a woman was finding it difficult to go to work each day because one of her co-workers frequently made cutting remarks to her, she was unable to think quickly enough to give any suitable response, and so she always ended up feeling humiliated.

I asked her how she would feel about talking with her co-worker, explaining her discomfort, trying to find out why she was being treated this way, and seeing if the two of them could work out some resolution in a dignified way. She said that she had tried this but had only received some cutting comment about her inability to take a joke.

I suggested that maybe she could develop a few stock responses, practice them in her imagination, and then, not having to think quickly about a response, snap off one of them whenever the occasion arose. She came up with something like, "If you're feeling so insecure that you find it necessary to belittle others, I understand." Then, in response to any other comment, she'd simply repeat, "Your insecurity is showing again."

She loved this idea and, thus armed, looked forward to going to work the next day. She reported that this simple maneuver has worked well for her.

Anger

Among the intense feelings that can disrupt a patient's abilities to think or act rationally, anger is common. Before constructive solutions can be found, it may be necessary to reduce the intensity of this feeling. There are clearly advantages to reducing it without blowups that would generate further complications.

If the anger seems unjustified by the circumstances that the patient describes, it may be important to help him/her realize that there are other ways of looking at the situation. This must be done with great care, lest the person feel that the therapist is just one more person who does not understand or is against him/her. Often, any attempts in this direction will be doomed to failure until the intensity of the emotion has been diminished.

Simply listening to the patient vent rage at some injustice, real or imagined, can be beneficial. A homework assignment will often work more effectively, is easier on the therapist, and is a technique that the patient can use independently forever after should the need arise. It sounds dumb, but it works very well.

The patient can be told to go home, find a quiet spot, and write the angriest, nastiest letter possible to the person(s) who made him/her so mad. It is to be totally uncensored, and is to be as profane, as cruel, or even as criminal as the patient's feelings dictate. It is to be neither a mere list of grievances nor an orderly entry into a journal; it's to be directed specifically to the target of his/her wrath.

Never, however, is the patient to let anyone else see it. It's not to be mailed or given to the other party. It's not to be hidden in some safe spot where it may be found "accidentally." It's not to leave his hands until he has finished it, read it over once, and then destroyed it completely.

I tell patients that I know it sounds stupid to spend so much time writing a letter that no one else will ever see, but that virtually every patient who has tried it has reported it as being very helpful. I add that I can't explain scientifically how it works, but it's almost as if the writing draws the anger out of the body and gets it onto the paper; then it can be thrown into the garbage. Of course, this is nothing more than another method of ventilation, but the patient can accomplish it without a facilitator and without an audience.

When the angry feelings are abated, patients do become more

capable of finding better solutions to their problems, either on their own or with the help of the therapist. Certainly they are less apt to leave a job in a rage, assault a rival, or make cruel accusations that could cause further problems in the future. They have a better chance of expressing their grievances to the appropriate party in a more constructive manner.

There is certainly much to be said for expressing anger directly to the one who caused it rather than using this indirect means. Consider just two reasons: First, letting the other person know about the anger may or may not feel good in itself, but keeping it contained always feels bad. Second, letting the other person know about the anger will frequently help stop some injustice that is occurring, or at least prevent its recurrence.

When, however, the one who evoked the anger is a hostile judge, an irate boss, or just big and mean, any pleasure derived from expressing the anger may be very short-lived. If the other person is deceased, direct communication is difficult, at best. If the patient hurls unbridled insults at a spouse, his chances of getting cheerful cooperation are not very great. Therefore, there are reasons for an indirect expression of anger.

When the source of the anger is a parent who is now dead, many patients are reluctant, initially, to use this technique, feeling that it is disloyal to write such ugly things to a deceased parent. Usually they can be helped to understand that the angry feelings are already there, that the parent will not be hurt by a letter that could never be delivered, even with an improved postal service, and that when the angry feelings have been dissipated there will once again be room for other, better feelings.

On page 00 I briefly described the silent abreaction as a hypnotic technique for reducing angry feelings. It works very well, but this ventilation via letter writing is so effective and requires so little time with the therapist that I now use letters much more often. It's my impression that they don't dissipate the anger quite as thoroughly as the silent abreaction, but I think there's an advantage to giving patients a tool they can use on their own.

Guilt

Guilt is another of the feelings that can impair a patient's abilities to find better solutions. The guilt may have been a long-standing feeling that preceded or even precipitated the incident, it may have arisen from the current traumatic incident, or it may not be present yet at all but exert its influence because the patient anticipates feeling guilty if s/he does those things which may be necessary for a better solution, like telling an adult child that s/he must return to school, get a job, or move out of the house.

Insight-oriented therapy may be indicated in some instances. If there has been a long-standing, pervasive feeling of guilt with no known source, I'd wish to analyze that symptom. If the patient says, "I know I shouldn't feel guilty about this, but I do anyway," I'd want to know why.

As an example of the latter instance, one patient had an alcoholic brother who had lost his job, so he and his alcoholic wife moved in with my patient and her husband. The two alcoholics did little during the day except drink and mess up the house while the other two were at work. At night, they merely went out to drink.

My patient knew that she shouldn't feel guilty about telling them to leave, but she did anyhow. A brief search for this "irrational" feeling revealed that, when she was a child, her mother was ill and was taken to the hospital, but before leaving extracted a promise that the patient would take care of her little brother. I explained that taking care of someone doesn't mean permitting them to continue with self-destructive behavior. It means helping them do those things that improve their lives. Giving them motivation to stop drinking would improve their lives, and about the only thing she hadn't tried to motivate them was telling them to stop drinking or move out. This enabled her to present such a demand. They moved out.

When the source of the guilt is known, symptom analysis is not needed. Examples would be: "My parents told me never to . . . ," or "I was taught in Sunday School that it was a sin to . . . , and even though I no longer believe that, the feelings are still there."

If, on the other hand, the source of any feeling is unknown, I personally prefer to use insight-oriented therapy. Here, however, we will be dealing primarily with guilt from some known, reasonable source, and will be talking about noninsight-oriented therapy for dealing with that guilt.

When the guilt has arisen from some real wrong that the patient has committed, there seems to be a poor response to sympathy or reassurance. The patient knows, or believes, that what he did was wrong and usually becomes engaged in some form of self-punishment. The self-punishment may be primarily mental, i.e., continued self-criticism with the resultant bad feelings that go along with that, or it may manifest itself in self-destructive behaviors of many different kinds. One way the therapist can aid the patient is by helping him/her understand that the punishment itself becomes a crime.

Usually it is easy to help patients see that the original victim of the wrongdoing receives no benefit from any self-inflicted punishment. Next, their own descriptions of what is transpiring allow them to realize that self-punishing behavior causes them to act in ways that are harmful not only to themselves but also to family, friends, employers, etc. When this has been accomplished, they can be given a better means of protecting themselves from the guilt – doing good things to make up for the bad ones that they had done before. This can even be compared to being sentenced to work furlough, if such a comparison would be helpful.

A couple of examples might help illustrate this idea. In the first, a young man had had an affair, confessed it to his wife, and after going through the upheaval that one might expect, was so consumed by guilt that when he was home he did virtually nothing other than sit around moodily, feeling remorseful about what he had done. It took virtually no time for me to help him see how this behavior was not helping his wife or children; in fact, they, the victims, were being made to suffer even more. I suggested that he sentence himself to spending some of his free time doing those things that would make them happier. Soon he was taking them out for picnics, to amusement parks, etc., and the whole family began feeling better, the patient included.

The second example is that of an almost courtly, middle-aged man who was so indoctrinated with "correct" manners that he would never enter my office ahead of me nor sit before I did. He had not been raised in this country, and almost seemed not to have been raised in this century. After he had resolved the original problem for which he had sought help, he blurted out that he felt so guilty he sometimes contemplated suicide.

He then told me that his mother had become chronically ill before her death. She had talked about nothing except her illness and was so demanding of attention that he could not stand it. He became impatient with her, acted rudely on occasion, and finally moved away so he would not have to put up with her anymore.

My talking about the normalcy of such behavior did nothing at all to help him in any visible way. (Although I know that sympathy and reassurance seldom ease this type of guilt, it still may be important for the patient to know that his behavior is normal.) I then went through the explanation about self-punishment causing pain to innocent victims and reparation being better than punishment. He was visibly relieved. He said, "I think that I could start donating some of my services to a charitable organization." He did, and his feelings of guilt diminished rapidly.

Dealing with anticipatory guilt follows pretty much the same principle, except here the "wrongdoing" has not yet occurred, so instead of giving the patient some way to make restitution, the therapist must help the patient see the positive value of doing what must be done.

As an example, a mother tells me that her 30-year-old son is still living at home. He gets jobs occasionally but loses them quickly because he doesn't get to work on time or doesn't go at all because he was out so late with his friends the night before. She knows that she shouldn't continue supporting this type of behavior, but if she made him move out of the house she couldn't live with her guilt. A very similar story is often told by wives of alcoholic husbands, or brothers, as in the earlier example.

The mother can be told that it's easy to understand how difficult it must be to tell her own son that he must leave the house, but unless she does so, she can expect him to continue acting the same way for many years to come, and he'll never learn to be a self-supporting adult. If she truly loves him and wants the best for him, she needs to make him see that his current behavior will no longer be tolerated, and that if he doesn't start behaving quite differently, he'll have to face very unpleasant consequences. Being tormented by her own concerns about his welfare may be a sacrifice that she'll need to make for his benefit.

The guilt is diminished by making this sacrifice in his behalf, but she then has to face a certain amount of realistic anxiety about his well-being when he is finally compelled to take care of his own needs. In my experience, the relief that comes from finally having him out quickly allays that anxiety.

This "shape up or ship out" approach can be modified a little to make it less harsh. He can be told that in one?, three?, or six? months at the maximum, he's to move out of the house, and unless he's found a job and kept it, he'll have no money for another place to stay. She loves him and cares about him, but because she does, she will no longer support a lifestyle that is destroying any hopes for his future.

Because this is such a difficult thing for most mothers to do, I believe that considerable support is needed, and so I refer such patients and their husbands to an organization called "Tough Love." This organization, originally designed as a self-help group for the parents of teenagers who become involved in drugs or other antisocial behaviors, appears to be very helpful for those parents who have difficulties in setting appropriate limits for their children of any age. When they hear the tales of other parents before and after setting such limits, the message I have tried to deliver becomes much more meaningful.

Grief

Grief also impairs a patient's ability to function well. When this feeling has arisen over the loss of a loved person, pet, or object, it can definitely blunt problem-solving capacities and thus lead to other complications. It is painful to all and can be almost overwhelming to those who seek our services because of it. Ventilation and time are necessary to reduce it significantly, and one of the therapist's customary tasks is to aid in the process of ventilation.

Budman and Gurman (1988, p. 88) state,

> As an initial therapeutic strategy, we believe that it is imperative to have the patient who has suffered the loss describe in as great detail as possible every aspect of the events leading to the loss. For example, Noreen, the physician whose father had committed suicide, was asked to detail everything that had happened in the days before the suicide and the days afterward. Such questions as "What went on during the phone conversation with your dad?", "Who said what?", "What did you do at that point?", and "What did you think and feel as you walked into your father's apartment?", were asked. To some degree, the detailed description of such events has almost a hypnogogic effect upon patients. As they begin to recall and search for significant details, many people take on the glazed, distant expression typical of those in an eyes-open trance state. Frequently, the regrieving may occur over a number of sessions, and at times, these sessions may be spaced by many months or even many years.

They also frequently advocate that the patient discuss the loss with other family members, and they may use other techniques to increase the emotional involvement as the loss is being discussed in the therapist's office. This would include the patient and therapist's looking together at photographs, home movies, diaries, etc. At times they also recommend visits to the gravesite.

Rarely is grief pure grief. Entangled, to varying proportions, are guilt, anger, and fear. Helping the patient to become more aware and gain control of those feelings enables healing to take place more quickly. Methods of dealing with anger and guilt were discussed earlier in this chapter; the same principles can still be applied when there is grief as well. Fear usually arises from the patient's concerns that s/he cannot survive in one way or another without the person who has been lost. Looking at the specific fears and helping him/her realize his/her own strengths and the availability of other resources helps to reduce these fears.

11 | HELP AFTER PAINFUL EMOTIONS HAVE BEEN RELIEVED

POWERFUL FEELINGS ARE not the only impediments to patients' finding appropriate solutions to their own problems. Often there are confusion and indecision arising from a variety of sources. One of these sources is the sad reality that in many instances there are no good solutions to be found, patients somehow believe they must find a good one, and thus their goals cannot be reached and they become confused by their failure.

In those cases, anything that patients do will have some painful consequences, and indecision serves as protection against the pain that they'll have to endure once a decision is made. Or conversely, each possible decision offers promise of good things to come, and going in one direction means losing the expected pleasures of going in another direction.

People rarely have trouble reaching a decision when one option is clearly better than the other, but when the choices are between a painfully demeaning job or no job, or between a wife who is loving, faithful, and comfortable or a new girlfriend who is selfish, immature, but exciting, making a choice can be an excruciating experience.

Relieving Indecision

In these cases I would rarely recommend one course of action over another, but it does help to clarify the situation by pointing out some simple truths. First, if all available options have been explored and it's seen that each will be painful, patients must be helped, very gently and with much empathy, to see that no good alternatives exist. They must make some difficult choices, and although any choice will be painful, making one will at least relieve them of the pain of indecision.

Next, they must be helped to fully understand the consequences of whatever actions they might be contemplating. Finally, it may help to point out the obvious: that although pain is never desirable, lesser pain is better than greater pain, briefer pain is better than longer pain, and when only bad choices are available, the one that is least bad is the best. I don't believe that pain necessarily makes one stronger, so that's one of the clichés I avoid.

Once patients understand the above, they often become able to make a decision. Even though they may be unhappy in their new situation, they then can begin the task of making the best of that situation.

An example follows. A woman whom I had been treating for other problems called my office in a state of great agitation. She had received a phone call from a doctor in a distant part of the state who had told her that her ex-husband was dying and that he wished to see their son. Her current husband was furious that she would even consider taking the son to see him, and there seemed to be no possibility of changing the husband's attitude. The son was too young to travel alone, and she knew no one else to make the journey with him.

I sympathized but told her that, unfortunately, no matter what she did, she would end up being unhappy. The question was, could she deal better with the guilt she would feel if she didn't take the son to see her ex-husband (who had treated her very badly in the past and had been negligent of the son until now) or with the anger that her current husband would display if she did make the trip?

The situation was clarified. She realized that there were no good choices to be made. She concluded that it would be better if she kept her present husband happy, even though she would have a certain amount of guilt to deal with in the future, and she calmed down almost immediately.

One of the major pitfalls with this tactic, and with the one to follow, is that many patients are unwilling to hear that there are no happy solutions to their problems. They come expecting us to create a happy ending. The timing and the tone with which the message is delivered are critical, and I do not always hit it right. When that happens, the patient drops out of therapy with me and sometimes seeks another therapist in our clinic. Recently, one of the other therapists told me that she had just seen a former patient of mine. "She said she really didn't have anything against Dr. Edelstien, but she just wanted to see someone else." This therapist added, "I believe the real trouble was that you told her what she had to hear."

I've not yet found a solution to this problem. This approach works well much of the time, and it seems to work more often as I've become increasingly sensitive to patients' pain. Still, there are failures, and when these occur, it's probably better to blame the way in which the technique was applied than to blame the patient for being unready to hear what she had to hear.

A second source of indecision is the patients' sense that there are too many possibilities with which to deal. In many cases it's useful to point out that there are only three: remaining in the current situation and continuing to endure the bitterness of it; changing the situation (or their attitude about it); or leaving the situation. As simple and obvious as this sounds, it often enables patients to lump what they thought were scores of possibilities into a mere three. They can begin studying the relative merits and disadvantages of those three, and soon orderly thinking begins to replace the chaotic.

This approach is quite similar to the one above, but all the possibilities are not necessarily painful, for changing the situation may prove pleasurable. Additionally, even though all of them may be difficult, the last two offer the possibility of better things to come, while the first virtually guarantees continued difficulties.

What happens when we work within the confines of these three possibilities? Rarely is the patient's life improved by deciding to stay and endure. Still, there are instances in which change cannot be effected because that would require the cooperation of someone who is unwilling to cooperate, and leaving would create problems greater than those currently being experienced. In those instances, coping with the situation must involve either finding ways to endure more comfortably and/or beginning to work toward goals that would permit leaving at some future time.

We see many cases of this type in our clinic, usually involving problems on the job or in a dreadful marriage. Let's look at the job situation for an example.

The patient has a job that has become virtually intolerable because of the workload, the time demands, or the insufferable attitude of others. The patient has developed multiple symptoms of anxiety and depression and is filled with anger as well. Attempts to change the situation at work have been tried and have failed. There are financial pressures, and without a steady paycheck a car would be repossessed, a home lost, or some other major difficulty would ensure.

The therapist may have tried to reduce the intensity of the anxiety and depression with medication or with psychological techniques. S/he may have tried to reduce the intensity of the anger with the "angry letter" technique. These efforts may have been successful in that the patient is now able to think more clearly about problem-solving.

He now realizes that he cannot change the situation, nor can he endure it forever, but leaving it, which before had seemed impossible, becomes a reality for some time in the future. He becomes able to see that he can begin looking for a new job in the same field while he holds on for a while to the old one. He might even begin night classes to learn skills that would permit him to enter a new job field. These solutions, which seem so obvious, were available to him all along, but the intensity of his feelings and his inability to sort out the three basic options interfered with his finding those solutions unassisted. There is almost always a great sense of relief once a viable option is recognized.

If, for whatever reasons, such plans cannot be made, ventilation and training in relaxation techniques make the enduring more tolerable. And, of course, in some instances, it's the patient's way of behaving on the job that is the main source of difficulty. If so, attempts must be made to help him find better ways of behaving, but this is unlikely to be successful until painful feelings have been diminished and alternatives have been examined.

Although there are only a few instances in which leaving the bad situation should be considered as the first of the three choices, there are times when I feel it is important to stand strongly on the side of that decision. If, for instance, a wife reports that her husband is drinking heavily, has abused her repeatedly in the past, and recently has been waving a loaded pistol while threatening to kill her, anything short of a strong recommendation to leave immediately is inadequate.

Her staying as long as she has may have been the only way she could imagine protecting herself against the dangers of leaving: the financial difficulties, threats from her husband if she goes, etc. She must be given a better protection against those dangers so she can better protect herself from the dangers of staying. Here, direct information about shelters for battered women, legal help, financial aid, and discussion of other alternatives can actually be life saving.

Perhaps it could be argued that such patients should be able to reach the decision to leave on their own, but when people have chronically suffered the stresses of a brutal marriage, when they have faced the recurrent anxiety of being beaten and threats of being killed, and when they have doubts about their abilities to survive on their own if they leave, such decisions are not made easily.

One might, instead, spend time analyzing why the patient has entered into such a marriage in the first place, why she has stayed in it so long, or why she is having such difficulty believing that she is capable of leaving, but that leads to the unpleasant possibility of having a patient who is partly analyzed and completely dead.

When the situation is less critical, there is much to be said for trying to change it before deciding to endure or to leave. This usually fits in more closely with the patient's hopes; and even when the tactic is unsuccessful, the patient is left with the knowledge that an earnest attempt was made before giving up. If the attempt is successful, then everyone is happier.

There's at least one other source of indecision, the patient's not knowing (or believing that s/he doesn't know) what is right, wrong, feasible, or not feasible. At times it's a true lack of knowledge, and when that's the case, the therapist should either convey the knowledge directly or tell the patient how to obtain it. For example, it's surprising that some patients believe that if they get a divorce they might lose custody of their children simply because they went to see a psychiatrist. It's sad to see that some women are afraid of a divorce because they don't realize that, instead of being penniless, they'd be entitled to half of the community property, alimony, and child support.

At times it's difficult to tell if it's a genuine lack of knowledge or a matter of "brain washing" that's being displayed. For example, I had a patient recently who wanted to leave her husband because of his continued drinking and abusive behavior, but all of her in-laws kept telling her that it was her fault that he drank (although he had started before he met her), it was her responsibility to take care of him, it would be her fault if he continued to deteriorate, etc.

At some level of awareness she knew that she was right and the in-laws were wrong, but so many voices criticizing her over such a long period made her question her own judgment. I strongly supported what she already knew was right, and that helped. However, I've found that group therapy is usually better for situations like that. The many, loud, angry voices of the group drown out the voices of the in-laws more quickly than my lone voice does.

Closely related to "not knowing" as a cause of indecision is the unfortunate habit of letting the other person make all the rules. We've seen a number of patients in our clinic who have spouses who separate from them, come back, separate again and again, or give messages like, "I'm gonna live with my new girlfriend now, and I don't know if I'll come back to you or not." The patient can't decide what to do, because she keeps waiting for him to tell her what he's going to do.

We try to make it very clear to these patients that, whenever someone lets the other person make all the rules, the first person always ends up losing. We try to help these patients gain the courage to make some of the rules themselves ("If you're not back home in 48 hours, I'm seeing an attorney!"), but this, too, is usually better done in a group setting where a whole chorus of voices can help bolster the courage.

Fostering Constructive Activity

Sometimes, the changes that one would like to see cannot be accomplished because that would require the cooperation of other, possibly unwilling parties. The boss may not be interested in offering a pay raise or in changing the work schedule; the husband may not see his drinking as a problem; the wife may continue buying new clothes with little regard to the family's finances; the children don't see anything wrong with leaving their clothes on the bedroom floor. In accord with the trauma theory, in accord with the principles of behavior therapy, in accord with the principles of strategic therapy, and most of all, in accord with everyday common sense, the patient then needs to find ways to increase the motivation of the other people concerned.

It's quite probable that anything that any of us does is done because we believe, consciously or otherwise, that doing this thing will make us feel better or prevent us from feeling worse. Those beliefs may be inaccurate at times, but we act on them anyway. The patient's task, then, becomes one of changing the other person's beliefs as to what would make that other person feel better or prevent him or her from feeling worse.

Before going into tactics to change the other person's beliefs, how-ever, the therapist should always explore the possibility that the pa-tient has failed to tell others what it is that he or she would like. It is sad to see how many patients have always been the "Rock of Gibral-ter" in their families, always doing what was asked of them and never asking anything in return. These patients suffer quietly, believing that the others should recognize their needs without being told, or they feel ashamed to voice a request, fearing that (1) their rock-like image will be destroyed forever or (2) the others will collapse if they suspect the patient is not truly omnipotent.

These patients should always be helped to make their wishes explic-it. While this is not always easy, there are at least two tactics, not mutually exclusive, which can be used. First, it's helpful to have them explore their concepts of the frailties of those for whom they have so much concern and to let them see how badly they have exaggerated those frailties. The exaggerations are usually the result of early child-hood experiences in which the others actually were in a greatly weakened state or were perceived to be in one. The continuation of that perception is often an exploitation of the patient to continue receiving his/her support, or an exploitation by the patient to contin-ue receiving kudos for being so supportive.

Next, patients benefit from an explanation that unless they manage to take care of themselves, they will not have the resources with which to take care of others. Seeing the call for help as a sign of intelligence and as an honest attempt to regain their own strengths makes it easier for them to ask.

At times, but rarely, the needs of the patient have not been met because the other people involved were simply too insensitive to recognize those needs, and once they are made known the necessary corrections are made. In any event, once the needs are made specific, the other party can never again claim, "I don't know why you're getting so upset about this. I thought you were happy with the way things were going."

In addition to getting the patient to ask for things, there is also the problem of getting these "rocks" to refuse to do things for others, even when the demands put upon them are clearly excessive. If the patient believes that saying "no" will irreparably damage a relationship, it is easy to point out that "If someone no longer likes you merely because you said 'no' in an appropriate way, then you haven't lost a friend, you've lost a parasite. You'll be better off." It's easy to point this out; it's not so easy for patients to put it into action. Most do, however, and they soon discover that it's really true. Those who are unable to say no, even when they realize that it should be said, are good candidates for insight-oriented therapy, and it can usually be found that they experienced some trauma when they said the forbidden word as a child.

Many patients are afraid of expressing their resentments about things because they fear that their anger, accumulated over long periods of silent resentment, will come out so strongly that others may be hurt. Their lack of speaking out can easily be seen as a means of protecting themselves from this danger. The danger can be reduced through ventilation via the "angry letter" techniques, and they can be taught better means of protecting themselves in the future rather than having to resort to the old solution of merely keeping quiet.

Simple education can provide them with a new protective mechanism: "If there's something that someone is doing and you don't like it, there's an easy three-step technique for letting them know what the problem is without criticizing or blaming them. First, compliment them, if you can do so honestly. Next, simply let them know what the problem is. Finally, offer a constructive solution while remaining open to an alternative solution.

"For example, if a friend is visiting and is upsetting you because he keeps dropping cigar ashes on your new carpet, you might say, 'Fred, I enjoy your company and I'm glad you dropped by to visit, but I'm afraid that one of those ashes might burn my new carpet. Would you mind using the ashtray on the table by your chair?'" Patients quickly learn that this simple technique works well and that the old dangers they imagined no longer exist.

An engineer was almost ready to leave his job because of a new supervisor who had taken charge of his unit and seemed to do so with more intensity than intelligence. Many complications had arisen. After hearing the example given above, the engineer approached his supervisor with, "I really admire the intensity with which you've worked on this project. It seems to me there may be a problem with . . . , however. Do you think we could fix it less expensively if we . . . ?" The response was far better than he had expected, and using the same technique repeatedly, the engineer found his job enjoyable once again. The supervisor was also happy, feeling flattered to be asked for his opinion by this skilled and experienced man.

With less formality than the three-step approach, the patient can be taught that merely telling the other person what is desired, rather than criticizing him for what is wrong, often helps bring about the desired changes. After I had instructed one of my patients about this, she came back the next week with a marvelous example of putting it into action.

Her husband played golf each weekend and apparently was sweaty and smelly when he returned. She found this highly objectionable, but he was not a man who took criticism easily. She told him, "Honey, you'd be even nicer to be with if you used an underarm deodorant before you played golf." She enjoyed the sweet smell of success.

If the patient has made his/her wishes clearly known and the other party is unwilling to meet the requests, then it becomes necessary to change the other party's motivation. When undesirable behavior is accepted, and particularly when it's rewarded in one way or another, one can usually expect to see much more of it. If any behavior is rewarded, one can generally expect to see much more of it. We know this from behavior therapy, from the corollary of the trauma theory, and we knew it before we knew about either of those technical ideas. We have known it since we were given gold stars for doing good work in the first grade or since we first got what we wanted by throwing a temper tantrum.

Although we know it, and our patients do too, they often lose sight of it because they are fearful that something bad will happen if they start utilizing this elegantly simple principle. It is useful to remind them.

Once reminded, patients can be helped to find ways of putting this principle into practice. Many patients, though, are hesitant to put anything new into practice. For months, or perhaps years, they've been sitting around wishing that the other person would change. When that's the case, I remind them of something else that they really know but have been denying: If *they* don't do something to change things, things are unlikely to change, except for the worse. Or, as one of my patients expressed it more colorfully, if less delicately, "My mother always told me, 'You can wish in one hand and spit in the other; see which one gets full first'."

Since the reward for good behavior is more effective, generally, and certainly more pleasant than the punishment for bad behavior, the initial efforts should be made to find new ways of encouraging better responses in a positive manner. When this fails, then the unpleasantness of "negative reinforcement" (behavior therapy jargon for "punishment") begins.

Simple examples of this might be: if a spouse or children leave dirty clothes lying on the bedroom floor, expecting the patient to pick them up, the patient simply lets them stay on the floor until they rot. Actually, I've never heard of a case in which the clothes lay around long enough to rot; once the offender has run out of clean ones, things start changing.

Or, if a spouse or children frequently come late for a meal, never notifying the cook in advance, the cook merely serves the meal at the expected time, then clears the table, letting offenders go hungry or fend for themselves. Few offenders go hungry or fend for themselves very long before changes start occurring.

The sequence of changes is fairly predictable. Initially there will be cries of outrage and angry accusations aimed at the patient. It is therefore important to warn the patient of this and let him know that the offender will try to reestablish the old status quo by inducing guilt or other unpleasant feelings. Forewarned, the patient may even be able to smile, at least inwardly, at this expected behavior.

If the patient is able to maintain his/her new stance, there is a second change. The other person grudgingly starts doing whatever proper behavior is indicated until the patient's guard is down, and then reverts to old patterns again. If forewarned, the patient immediately reverts to his/her own new behavior in response to the other person's old behavior. With luck and perseverance, this brings about the third stage, which is continued better response from the other person. More often, stages one and two must be endured several times before stage three is stabilized.

Although I believe that deliberately making someone else feel bad is one of the quickest ways to ruin a relationship, when more gentle approaches have not worked the punishment strategy may be the only resource left to improve the relationship. If simple punishments like the ones above do not work, more forceful ones may be tried. If those fail, then the patient is left with only two options—to endure or to leave.

If the patient is truly willing to leave if things do not improve, and only when that decision has been firmly reached, a statement to that effect can be made in one last effort to promote change. For example, "The next time you come home drunk, I'm seeing an attorney and getting a divorce." Or, "If you ever hit me again, I'm calling the police, and you're going to jail."

When such threats are truly sincere, the offending party seems to recognize the sincerity, so such threats never should be made as bluffs, and they must be followed through. If they don't help establish better behavior, then leaving the situation becomes the only viable option.

Overview

If we use the trauma theory for understanding and treating those psychological disorders with obscure origins we find:

1. The patient experienced a traumatic incident.
2. S/he experienced painful feelings as a result of that incident.
3. S/he adopted symptomatic behavior to avoid recurrence of the painful feelings.
4. Therapy helps him/her develop better methods of protection or understand that the old dangers no longer exist.

We can use the same theory for those psychological disorders with obvious origins, but:

1. We see the patient while the traumatic incident is still occurring or shortly after it occurred.
2. The painful feelings are the "symptoms" of the adjustment disorder.
3. Therapy is essentially the same as noted above, but now it can prevent the adoption of symptomatic behavior.
4. To facilitate this therapy we must first remove those things that are impeding the patient from finding his own solutions:
   (a) the intensity of the painful feelings must be reduced;
   (b) clarification must replace confusion about options available;
   (c) self-determined action must replace indecisiveness and wishful thinking.

These are the relatively uncomplicated steps of the relatively uncomplicated therapy that is made possible by using the uncomplicated trauma theory. In the next section we shall look at those disorders that (probably) arise primarily from biological trauma to the patient.

IV | *DISORDERS OF BIOLOGICAL ORIGIN*

12 | RECOGNIZING WHEN PSYCHOTHERAPY WON'T HELP

IN EARLIER SECTIONS I alluded to the fact that there are differences in the theoretical frameworks that different therapists apply to the same illnesses. For the most part, these differing opinions all apply to differing beliefs regarding the psychological origins of the problems. In this section, we will see that the differences are even greater, for here we are faced with the proposition that some therapists believe there is a psychological basis for some conditions which other therapists believe are primarily physiological.

The two cannot be entirely separated, of course, for emotional changes produce physiological changes and many physiological changes produce emotional responses. Very simple examples would be: sudden fright will cause a rapid heart beat, while an unexpected rapid heart beat, as in paroxysmal tachycardia, may cause the person to feel extremely frightened. But even while understanding that the two cannot be entirely separated, there is reason to believe that some of the conditions we treat are much more heavily influenced by biological factors than by emotional ones.

I am not going to write about biological therapies by describing specific medications, doses, pharmacokinetics, etc. There is enough written about that each year to satisfy anyone, except the authors of more such material. Instead, I will offer observation and speculation.

Initially, I wondered if I should write a whole section that is nothing more than observation and speculation. On brief reflection, I realized that observation and speculation comprise the whole content of any book on psychotherapy.

I will start, then, with what might be the wildest of my speculations. Could it be true that any of the "psychological" disorders that do not respond, most of the time, to brief therapy (and some of them that do) are really disorders of physiological origin?

There is no solid evidence that this is true, but there have been numerous examples in which it seems to be true. Despite the wonderful psychological (mostly analytic) theories to explain a number of disorders, many that do not respond well to brief therapy methods have been shown to be of physiological origin. A partial list would include: schizophrenia, manic-depressive disorder, at least some of the unipolar depressions, obsessive compulsive disorder, alcoholism, and panic disorder.

The "proof" is not as conclusive as we might like it to be, but it is certainly more solid than that offered by those who claim these disorders are the result of early childhood experiences. My purpose in going to some length to point this out is to demonstrate that, no matter how profound and intellectually stimulating a theory might be, we must constantly guard against accepting it merely because some esteemed authority has presented it to us.

We should also guard against believing the "scientific" physical theories too quickly, but when the evidence weighs more heavily toward one side than the other, even though we cannot be certain, it makes sense for us to lean toward the side with the weightier evidence. Certainly, when the physical therapies are recognized as being more effective than the psychological therapies, we should apply the physical. I will now offer two examples.

The examples are taken from the works of two men whose writings I've admired. Their writings display superior intelligence, profound knowledge of their craft, and skillful application of that knowledge. At the time they wrote their books there was not as much known about biological factors as we know now, so they were compelled to work with the best theory then available, the psychoanalytic theory. Let's see how that theory holds up in the light of current knowledge. Greenson (1967) writes (p. 19):

> Some years ago a young woman, Mrs. A., came for treatment accompanied by her husband. She complained that she was unable to leave her house alone and felt safe only with her husband. In addition, she complained of a fear of fainting, a fear of dizziness, and a fear of becoming incontinent. Mrs. A.'s symptoms had begun quite suddenly some six months earlier while she was in a beauty parlor.
>
> The analysis, which lasted several years, revealed that the actual trigger for the outbreak of the patient's phobias was the event of having her hair combed by a male beautician. We were able eventually to uncover the fact that at that moment she was reminded of her father combing her hair when she was a little girl. The reason she had gone to the beauty parlor that day was her pleasurable expectation of seeing her father, who was to visit the young married couple for the first time since their marriage. He was to stay in their home and she was filled with great delight, consciously. However, unconsciously, she was full of guilt feelings for loving her father and for her predominantly unconscious hostility toward her husband.
>
> The apparently innocuous event of having her hair combed stirred up old incestuous longings, hostilities, guilt, and anxiety. To put it briefly, Mrs. A. had to be accompanied by her husband in order to be sure he had not been killed by her death wishes. Also his presence protected her from acting out sexually. The fears of fainting, of dizziness, and of incontinence were symbolic representations of losing her moral balance, losing her self-control, soiling her good character, humiliating herself, and falling from her high position. The young woman's symptoms had links to the pleasurable body sensation of childhood as well as to infantile punishment fantasies.
>
> I believe one can formulate the events as follows: the combing of her hair stirred up repressed id impulses which brought her into conflict with her ego and superego. Despite the absence of obvious neurotic symptoms prior to the outbreak of the phobias, there were indications that her ego already was relatively depleted and her id lacked adequate discharge possibilities. Mrs. A. had had difficulty in

sleeping for years, nightmares, and inhibitions in her sexual life. As a consequence the fantasies mobilized by the hair combing increased the id tensions to a point where they flooded the infantile defenses of the ego and involuntary discharges took place, eventuating in acute symptom formation.

Today, I believe that most clinicians would diagnose the young lady as having a panic disorder with agoraphobia. Many of us would think that the psychoanalytic formulations, if true at all, were totally irrelevant. We would believe that her illness is of biologic origin. Her fears of fainting and of dizziness were absolutely typical of panic disorder, and the sudden onset of her symptoms in the beauty parlor was a mere coincidence, for the symptoms could just as easily have started in her car, in the supermarket, or anywhere else (as such symptoms do start in many people with this disorder).

We would believe that the agoraphobia was a direct result of the sudden panic attack and was the result of her fear that she would have another attack away from her home and alone; thus the need to have her husband with her.

I further believe it's sad that during the several years of her analysis she had to deal with guilt about loving her father and fear that her husband might be killed by her death wishes, but such is the material that comes out of a classical analysis. I strongly suspect that these painful feelings were the product of the analysis itself. Even if those feelings were not the product of the analysis but existed on their own at some subconscious level, I suspect that they could have been allowed to remain subconscious and she would have felt better during those few years with no residual harm.

One might claim that her poor sleep and her lack of sexual desire were the result of these subconscious feelings, but I believe that there is an equally plausible explanation, although there's not enough clinical data in this brief presentation to support or refute my speculation: The poor woman was also depressed. We know that a significant percentage of patients with panic disorder also have a depression (Grunhaus, 1988; Leckman, Weissman, Merkangas, et al, 1983), so there's at least a significant chance that this diagnosis is correct. We also know that disruption of sleep patterns and diminished libido are frequent findings in depressed patients, so there's a little more evidence to support that diagnosis. My main point, though, is that there is ample reason to consider possibilities other than these analytic formulations.

The second example is presented by Dewald (1972). He writes (p. 11),

> The major symptoms began in the last month of her first pregnancy and consist of acute attacks of free-floating anxiety accompanied by palpitations, sweating, a sense of dread and terror, and at times a fear of dying. . . . She also has a variety of phobias particularly involving being alone. . . . She has fears of death. . . . At times she fears that she will not be able to breathe. . . . She also has episodes of moderately severe depression.

Before we go any further, let me review briefly what *DSM-III* has to say about the symptoms of panic disorder, so the reader can compare this with the two cases:

> Panic attacks are manifested by discrete periods of apprehension or fear, and at least four of the following symptoms appear during each attack: dyspnea (difficulty breathing); palpitations; chest pain or discomfort; choking or smothering sensations; dizziness, vertigo, or unsteady feelings; feelings of unreality; tingling in hands or feet; hot and cold flashes; sweating; faintness; trembling or shaking. (p. 231)

I would feel confident in diagnosing this case, too, as panic disorder and depression, the latter based upon Dewald's statement that she has episodes of moderately severe depression. Most of my comments about the first case would also apply here. I will not go through the entire "synthesis" of the case that Dewald offers; let's just look at his explanation of her fears of dying:

> Her fears of dying, choking, being unable to breathe, and her fear of going to sleep were derivative manifestations of the oral conflicts with the unconscious equation of each of these activities with suckling

at the breast and the various fantasied dangers elaborated as part of the oral triad. In these various symptomatic experiences she was unconsciously gratifying the fantasy of nursing and of being devoured by the breast, while at the same time experiencing this as a dangerous and anxiety-provoking situation and as an ego-alien fear which interfered with normal functions. In the fear of death she was also unconsciously equating orgasm with dying, so that this fear also had meaning for her as a defense against the prohibited sexual gratification.

These explanations may sound either intriguing or like pure nonsense, depending upon one's own orientation, but today we do have other available explanations.

Let's also note that in the Epilogue to the case, E. James Anthony, M.D., writes, "This patient was analyzed, by present-day criteria, in 'a remarkably short time' (two years: 347 hours: $14^1/_2$ days!), and the question that arises is, what made this possible?"

Two years? Three hundred forty-seven sessions? I would ask, instead, what made this permissible? It was permissible, and perhaps even necessary, because in 1972 we did not know about the biology of panic disorders. I don't believe we even had the diagnosis then, and the analytic theory may have been the best theory available. Today, it would seem inexcusable to treat a similar patient in a similar way, and as we shall see shortly, this analytic theory crumbles again and again as biological sciences have provided us with new information.

Today, the evidence for panic disorder being a biological disorder is certainly more persuasive than the theoretical formulations that were used so imaginatively in the two volumes quoted above. We now know that if panic disorder patients are given injections of sodium lactate, most of them will have a panic attack almost immediately, while only a small percentage of patients without this diagnosis (yet) will respond in similar fashion (Hollander et al., 1989). We know the same thing is true if both groups are given inhalations of carbon dioxide (Woods et al., 1988). Positron Emission Tomography has demonstrated blood flow asymmetry in the parahippocampal gyrus, indicating that some sort of physiological abnormality is present.

And, to further bolster the belief that this is a biological disorder, genetically transmitted, Crowe (1985) reviewed a number of studies which showed that two-thirds of cases have relatives affected with the same condition; that the risk to first-degree relatives is approximately three to four times the rate of the general population; and that twin studies report a 30–40% concordance in identical twins compared to the 0–4% in fraternal twins.

The most efficient treatment today is biological. Antidepressants, including both the tricyclics and the MAO inhibitors, and a specific minor tranquilizer, alprazolam, all offer the great majority of cases relatively prompt and complete relief from the panic attacks.

This treatment can provide freedom from attacks within a few weeks in some cases, while it may take a few months in others. The relief, however, is not always permanent, for it is now believed that this is a chronic, recurring illness, and perhaps 50% or more of patients will have future attacks even after complete freedom from them for a year or more.

I know of no statistics to show what percentage of patients have recurrence of attacks after psychoanalysis for this disorder. On the other hand, I know of no statistics showing that psychoanalysis helps at all, for although the individuals treated by Greenson and Dewald apparently recovered from their attacks, many people have spontaneous remissions within the period of time that the analyses took.

Depression

I will begin with a very personal experience learning about and treating this disease. When I was taking a psychiatric residency (1966–69), we were taught that "neurotic depressions" were the result of early childhood experiences and that the proper treatment was the uncovering of these experiences and resolution of the feelings generated by them. It was not uncommon to believe such theoretical offerings as those offered by Dewald in the previously mentioned case when he talked about the origin of that patient's depression: " . . . The depression was also the result of the inevitable frustration of her childhood fantasies and yearnings, particularly those related to her phallic wishes and those connected to the demands for oedipal and pre-oedipal satisfactions. These depressive responses to infantile and childhood frustration were particularly manifest in the transference neurosis during the termination phase of the analysis."

I, like my fellow residents, believed what we were taught, although I don't believe that we ever actually had patients who expressed such phallic wishes and demands for oedipal and pre-oedipal satisfactions. We assumed that we did not see these because we were doing analytically oriented psychotherapy instead of true psychoanalysis, and perhaps we were not doing the former very well.

Fortunately, we were also taught that if our patients had not shown significant improvement within a couple of months, we might consider giving them antidepressant medication while we continued our exploration of the "deep, underlying dynamics of their depressions." We were cautioned to offer these medications with comments like, "Maybe this will help you feel a little better while we continue the important work at hand." Presumably this was to avoid the horror of a patient's feeling better because of placebo effect and to clearly underline the superiority of the psychological treatment. Certainly we were taught that the antidepressants would only mask the symptoms and not treat the underlying disease at all.

Believing what I had been taught, I started practicing what I believed. My observation was that almost every patient showed improvement by the second or third week, but as we continued our search for the deep underlying causes, that improvement diminished and the depression persisted, at varying intensities. Then, after a couple of months, I would prescribe antidepressant medications, and the patient would feel better and function better as we continued our therapeutic task.

After a while—too long a while for me to feel proud of it—I asked myself, since I was putting virtually all of my depressed patients on an antidepressant anyway, why not put them on it early and let them feel better while we did the "real" work?

Following this, I had patients who felt much less depressed much more quickly, but we persisted in looking for the cause of the depression for another six months, twelve months, two years, or until the patient moved to another city or had the sense to stop treatment. Some of them, of course, were able to "find the cause of their depressions," resolve the feelings, and terminate therapy with the shared illusion that we had accomplished something valuable. All of them were able to uncover old hurts, and we discussed these at length, with the sense of learning important things about the patient, but often with no clinical changes.

In regard to the patients who clearly improved, some of them had relapses that I knew about, for they returned for further therapy, and others, I'm sure, had relapses that I never knew about.

In 1980, I joined an HMO. Because of the flood of patients who came there seeking psychotherapy, often I could not schedule a follow-up appointment after the intake interview for about two weeks. When the initial interview permitted me to feel confident that depression was the correct diagnosis, I would start the antidepressant at that visit and plan to start "real therapy" approximately two weeks later.

A fascinating thing occurred. Patient after patient came back with approximately the same report, "Doc, I still have all the problems that I came in with, but I feel like my old self again, and I believe I can take care of them the way I used to."

I, believing that this was merely a resistance to uncovering traumatic material, was highly dubious, but cautiously agreed to follow them for medication only, unless they decided that they'd like to explore more deeply the origins of their illness.

I soon discovered that these patients did better than the ones I had seen in private practice, for whom "insight" had been the primary treatment and medication had been a mere supplement. I had another of my "wild" speculations: "Does insight-oriented therapy prolong depression?" After all, it's pretty hard to think about, talk about, and even dream about old depressing incidents for months at a time without feeling depressed in the process. Had I been a better student of Shakespeare, I might have wondered about this sooner, for he realized long before I did that, "Those who summon up remembrances of things past grieve at grievances foregone."

But a number of patients had indeed experienced very traumatic and depressing incidents in their lives, and when they first came in, their thoughts often were focused heavily on those events. Those were some of the kinds of events that I had been taught led to depressions, and wouldn't it be negligent to allow those events to remain undiscussed? I discovered that as the antidepressant medication relieved the depression, the patients still remembered the traumatic events but did not think of them often or suffer bad feelings when they did.

Another speculation: These unhappy childhood experiences may not have been the cause of the depression at all; the depression caused the ruminations about them. The grievances, indeed, were foregone, and the recurrent thoughts were a symptom of the depression, not a cause.

I had also been taught that low self-esteem was one of the building blocks of depression, that it was the result of improper parenting, and that the therapist had to help the patient deal with those issues. I found that virtually every depressed patient I saw had low self-esteem, but as the depression lifted the esteem rose, even in those who had had depression and low self-esteem for many years, often going back into their childhoods.

Speculation: Like ruminations about unhappy events, low self-esteem is more often the result of depression than the cause of it.

Not all depressed patients with low self-esteem felt good about themselves when the depression lifted, and I do believe that there are childhood experiences that can cause this symptom, as some of my case examples in Chapter 6 demonstrated. Still, I speculate that it is unwise to start working on that issue with "insight" until one sees if it's still an issue after the depression has been treated with medication.

Another one of my lessons about depression was that it was often the result of anger turned inward against the self instead of being directed toward some other person who actually deserved it. Certainly many of the patients I saw expressed a great deal of self-criticism, if not actual hatred of themselves. Many of them also had a great deal of animosity toward others; sometimes it was blatant, at other times thinly disguised.

Like the other symptoms mentioned, most of this would disappear as the depression did. It is no speculation that excessive self-criticism and increased irritability are common symptoms of depression.

In regard to that increased irritability, I will add a brief aside: Because antidepressants worked so well to relieve marked irritability in the depressed patients, we started trying them in our clinic for patients who had no symptoms other than increased irritability. This was often of marked proportions: women who were screaming constantly at their children and always angry with their husbands; men who would yell at their families over trivia and punch holes in walls or kick their feet through doors. They all said that they knew it was wrong even while they were doing it, but they just couldn't control themselves.

The results of the antidepressant medications were remarkable. I cannot offer solid statistics, for we do not have the time or manpower to do the research we would like, but I would estimate that in the 30–40 cases of which I am aware, excellent results were found in all but one or two.

The NIMH has found that the earliest effect of amitriptyline is reduction in feelings of hostility and anxiety. The researchers did not yet know if the effects would be the same for other tricyclics. In our clinic we have had good results in the reduction of hostility with trazodone, doxipin, protriptyline, and amitriptyline. I suspect that they'll discover the same thing, although the study cited was with depressed patients, and the patients about whom I'm writing are not necessarily depressed.

It is our speculation that this loss of temper control is also a familial disease, since almost all of our patients have reported that members of their families either had this or had depressions. One man, who was built like a locomotive and was someone I would not like to encounter when he went off track, reported that all the male members of his family were like this, and he could not visit with his father or brothers for more than 15 minutes without their getting into a fist fight. Within one week after starting trazodone, he reported, "I've turned into a pussycat. I don't let people walk over me, but my temper is under control, and my family and co-workers are amazed." Similar but less dramatic reports have been given by virtually all other patients. Unfortunately, each time any of them stops the medication, the symptoms return. The antidepressants, apparently, do not "cure" this malady any better than insulin cures diabetes; however, like insulin, they offer very gratifying control.

Modern research on the neurotransmitters gives us good reason to believe that, despite the old theories to the contrary, depression is most likely a biological disorder. Added to this evidence are family studies. Weissman and Boyd (1985) state,

> There is no question that depression is familial. A family history of depression doubles or triples the risk of depression. In several recent studies, the rate of major depression in the relatives of depressed probands was triple that of the relatives of normal probands, regardless of whether strict or loose criteria of depression were used in the relatives, and regardless of whether the proband was an ambulatory or hospitalized depressive. (p. 768)

Another clue that the disease is familial, on a biological basis rather than a "learned behavior" basis, is the clinical observation that almost always, if one member of a family has responded well to a certain antidepressant, other members of that family will respond well to exactly the same medication.

The old theories about depression have caused a lot of harm, in my estimation. We encounter many patients in our clinic who do not want to take medications; they want to "find the psychological cause" for their illness—despite the fact that a number of them have had years of insight-oriented therapy without any benefit at all. Still, they have heard about the old theories (often from their prior therapists) and believe that this is the only acceptable therapeutic approach.

It is often difficult to convince these patients otherwise, but explaining the biological theory to them and offering them literature to take home and read often help. The greatest help comes from having them enter one of our crisis groups, where we almost always have one to three patients who started an antidepressant one or two weeks before and who declare, "I didn't want to use medications either, but I decided to give them a try, and I can't believe how much better I feel now."

The greatest harm, I believe, comes from the fact that many therapists still give credence to the old theories, and that's why we see so many patients who've had years of therapy with no improvement. The relatively newer psychological treatments, like cognitive-behavioral and interpersonal therapies, have a good track record, and if they take twelve weeks or so to produce the same benefits we often see in one to two weeks with medication, that's not a huge difference. Those therapies may even have an advantage, since the medication patients must stay on their medications for at least six months. It seems unconscionable, though, to subject any patient to years of insight-oriented therapy without significant change.

Manic-Depressive Disorder

Although I'd assume that all psychiatric residents who have had their training in the last 10–15 years have never considered this disorder to be anything other than a physiological one, it is still interesting to see what was being written about it only 30 years ago, and what was being taught about it only 20 years ago. Arieti (1959) writes:

> Freud, in a paper titled "Mourning and Melancholia," accepted Abraham's ideas that there is a relation between mourning and melancholia and pointed out that, whereas in mourning the object is lost because of death, in melancholia there was an internal loss because the lost person had been incorporated. The sadism present in the ambivalent relationship is then directed against the incorporated love-object.

This concept of introjection helped Freud to develop the concepts of ego-ideals and later, of super-ego. In a subsequent work published in 1921 (*Group Psychology and the Analysis of the Ego*), Freud advanced the idea that in mania there is a fusion between the ego and the super-ego. Thus the energy previously used in the conflict between the two parts of the psyche is now available for enjoyment. Freud also pointed out that this fusion between ego and super-ego may be based on biologically determined cycles (something similar to the cyclic fusion of the ego and id, which periodically occurs every night during the state of sleep).

In later works Abraham confirmed Freud's findings and clearly postulated the factors which are prerequisites for manic-depressive psychosis: 1) a constitutional and inherited overaccentuation of oral erotism; 2) a special fixation of the libido on the oral level; 3) a severe injury to infantile narcissism, brought about by disappointments in love; 4) the occurrence of this disappointment before the Oedipus complex was resolved; and 5) the repetition of the primary disappointment in later life.

After Abraham and Freud, Rado and Melanie Klein have, perhaps, made the most important psychoanalytic contributions to this subject. For Rado, "melancholia is a despairing cry for love." The ego tries to punish itself in order to prevent the parental punishment. The patient attempts to repeat the sequence—guilt, atonement, forgiveness—which, according to Rado, is connected with a previous sequence occurring in the infant—wakening, rage, hunger, appearance of the mother's breast, and ensuing satisfaction. The excitement of being nursed by the mother is compared to a sexual orgastic experience, and mania is compared to an oral fusion, an equivalent of the breast situation. (p. 422)

As in depression and panic disorder, this inventive theorizing seems to crumble as we have become more knowledgeable about the biological nature of manic-depressive disorder. To the best of my knowledge, no one has yet found a cure for this disease, but at least it is usually very controllable with medication, but not with therapy based upon these analytic concepts. Of course, manic-depressive disorder does not make patients immune to other problems, and counseling of one form or another may be indicated to help them deal with problems in their lives. Yet, complicated theory leading to complicated therapy is once again virtually useless.

Other Disorders

The theory of the "refrigerator mother" gave a psychological explanation for childhood autism; as a consequence, some untold number of mothers were subjected to horrible guilt about inflicting this terrible disease on their children. There is no evidence that this theory produced a therapy that was beneficial to the patient. Modern thought is that autism is a biological disorder.

The theory of the schizophrenogenic mother was offered to explain schizophrenia, and again, an untold number of mothers were subjected to needless guilt. Although it is true that many of these mothers do have patterns of speech that are disturbing to anyone who listens to them, and indeed may put their children into "double bind" situations in which anything the child does is wrong, there is fairly substantial evidence that schizophrenia is primarily a biological disorder, genetically transmitted. If this be true, then it is easy to speculate that the mothers who speak and act in the aforementioned manners do so because they have inherited a much milder version of the thought disorder.

There have been heroic attempts to treat schizophrenics according to psychoanalytic theories. Antipsychotic medication and supportive therapy do a better job.

We have had the theories of anal fixations to explain obsessive compulsive disorders. It is looking significantly more probable that this is another physiological disorder.

We have had explanations about the oral fixations and dependencies that lead to alcoholism. It is more likely that there is a genetically transmitted error of metabolism that creates the craving for alcohol once the potential alcoholic has had his exposure to alcohol and, of course, many alcoholics have also had to endure the psychological impact of being raised by alcoholic parents. It is easy to speculate that the dependency which these patients display is a result of their alcoholism rather than a cause of it.

No therapy based upon analytic theories has worked as well for the alcoholic as has the therapy developed by Alcoholics Anonymous.

In summary, there has never been any substantial proof for any of the complicated analytic theories about any of these illnesses, and there is a growing body of evidence that indicates that these theories are either totally wrong or completely irrelevant. Certainly, they have not produced therapies that are useful.

If the complicated theories of infantile fixations, fantasies, and drives are discredited in the aforementioned illnesses, then one must begin to wonder why therapists today still give credence to them in any illness. None of these complicated theories has ever been proven, and they lead to therapies that are horrendously long and frightfully expensive. The simpler theories are equally unproven, but they lead to briefer therapy that seems to work at least as well, and now that modern medications exist, as imperfect as they may be, we can offer control, if not cure, for some of the most painful of the "psychological" disorders, which never responded well to psychological intervention.

Perhaps Tolstoy understood why therapists still cling to the complicated theories. He is quoted by Gleick (1988, p. 38):

> I know that most men, including those at ease with problems of the greatest complexity, can seldom accept even the simplest and most obvious truth if it be such as would oblige them to admit the falsity of conclusions which they have delighted in explaining to colleagues, which they have proudly taught to others, and which they have woven, thread by thread, into the fabric of their lives.

A Final Word

I have not written a conclusion, for I feel strongly that each of you should draw your own. Although we can hardly call psychiatry a science, we should strive in the direction of making it one, and in that regard, I like the words of Carl Sagan (1980, p. 16), "Science is based on the experiment, on a willingness to challenge old dogma, on an openness to see the universe as it really is. Accordingly, science sometimes requires courage—at the very least the courage to question conventional wisdom."

REFERENCES

Adler, G. (1986). Psychotherapy of the narcissistic personality disorder patient: Two contradictory approaches. *American Journal of Psychiatry*, 143:4, 430–436.

Alexander, F., & French, T. M. (1974). *Psychoanalytic therapy: Principles and application*. Lincoln: University of Nebraska Press.

Alexander, F. (1965). Psychoanalytic contributions to short-term psychotherapy. In L. R. Wolberg (Ed.), *Short-term psychotherapy*, New York: Grune and Stratton.

American Psychiatric Association. (1980). *Diagnostic and statistical manual of mental disorders (3rd ed.)*. Washington, DC: Author.

American Psychiatric Association. (1987). *Diagnostic and statistical manual of mental disorders (3rd ed. revised)*. Washington, DC: Author.

Andrews, G., & Harvey, R. (1981). Does psychotherapy benefit neurotic patients? *Archives of General Psychiatry*, 38.

Arieti, S. (1959). Manic-depressive psychosis. In S. Arieti (Ed.), *American Handbook of Psychiatry, Vol. 1*. New York: Basic Books.

Baker, H., & Baker, M. (1987). Heinz Kohut's self psychology: An overview. *American Journal of Psychiatry*, 144:1, 1–9.

Beitman, B., Goldfried, M., & Norcross, J. (1989). The movement toward integrating the psychotherapies: An overview. *American Journal of Psychiatry*, 146:2, 138–147.

Bornstein, B. (1977). The analysis of a phobic child. In S. Morce & R. Watson, (Eds.), *Psychotherapies, a comparative casebook*. New York: Holt, Rinehart and Winston.

Budman, S., & Gurman, A. (1988). *Theory and practice of brief therapy*. New York: Guilford.

Burdick, D. (1975). Rehabilitation of breast cancer patients. *Cancer*. 36:645–648.

Burgess, A., & Holstrom, L. (1974). Rape trauma syndrome. *American Journal of Psychiatry*, 131:981–985.

163

Cheek, D., & LeCron, L. (1968). *Clincal hypnotherapy*. New York: Grune and Stratton.

Clinical Psychiatry News. (1987). Reduced anxiety, hostility early effect of tricyclics. 15:3.

Cooper, A. (1983). The place of self psychology in the history of depth psychology. In A. Goldberg (Ed.), *The future of psychoanalysis*. New York: International Universities Press.

Crews, F. (1986). *Skeptical engagements*. New York: Oxford University Press.

Crowe, R. (1985). The genetics of panic disorder and agorophobia. *Psychiatric Developments*, 2:171–186.

de Shazer, S. (1985). *Keys to solutions in brief therapy*. New York: W. W. Norton.

de Shazer, S. (1988). *Clues: Investigating solutions in brief therapy*. New York: W. W. Norton.

Dewald, P. (1972). *The psychoanalytic process: A case illustration*. New York: Basic Books.

Edelstien, M. G. (1981). *Trauma, trance and transformation: A Clinical Guide to Hypnotherapy*. New York: Brunner/Mazel.

Edelstien, M. G. (1982). Ego state therapy in the management of resistances. *American Journal of Clinical Hypnosis*, 25:1.

Eichelman, B. (1987). Neurochemical basis of aggressive behavior. *Psychiatric Annals*, 17:6.

Ellis, A. (1977). The treatment of a psychopath with rational psychotherapy. In S. Morse, & R. Watson (Ed.), *Psychotherapies: A comparative casebook*. New York: Holt, Rinehart, and Winston.

Fiore, E. (1988). Presentation at the San Francisco Academy of Hypnosis.

Freud, S. (1896). The aetiology of hysteria. *Standard Edition* 3:191–221. New York: Norton, 1953.

_____(1909). *Analysis of a phobia in a five-year-old boy, Standard Edition*, 10:5–147. New York: Norton, 1953.

_____(1928). Dostoiesvski and parricide. *Standard Edition* XXI. New York: Norton, 1953.

Freud, S. (1954). *The origins of psychoanalysis: Letters to Wilheim Fliess, Drafts and Notes 1887–1902*. M. Bonaparte, & A. Freud (Eds.). New York: Basic Books.

Freud, S. (1937). Analysis terminable and interminable. *Standard Edition*, 23. New York: Norton.

Freud, S., & Jung, C. (1974). *The Freud/Jung letters: The correspondence between Sigmund Freud and Carl G. Jung*. McGuire, W. (Ed.). Princeton: Princeton University Press.

Fyer, N., Uy, J., Martinez, J., Goetz, R., Klein, F., Fyer, A., Liebowitz, M., & Gorman, J. (1987). CO 2 challenge of patients with a panic disorder. *American Journal of Psychiatry*, 144:8.

Garfield, S., & Bergin, A. (1978). *Handbook of psychotherapy and behavior change*.

Gleick, J. (1988). *Chaos: Making a new science*. New York: Penguin Books.

Goodman, D. (1986). Genetic factors in the development of alcoholism. *Psychiatric Clinics of North America*, 9:3.

Goulding, M. & Goulding, R. (1979). *Changing lives through redecision therapy*. New York: Brunner/Mazel.

Greenson, R. (1967). *The technique and practice of psychoanalysis*, 1. New York: International Universities Press.

Grunbaum, A. (1984). *The foundation of psychoanalysis: A philosophical critique*. Berkeley: University of California Press.

Grunhaus, L., (1988). Clinical and psychobiological characteristics of simultaneous panic disorder and major depression. *American Journal of Psychiatry*, 145:1214–21.

Gurman, A., & Kniskern, D. (1978). Research on marital and family therapy. In Garfield, & Bergen (Eds.), *Handbook of Psychotherapy and Behavior Change*.

Gustafson, J. (1986). *The complex secret of brief psychotherapy*. New York: W. W. Norton.

Haley, J. (Ed.) (1985). *Conversations with Milton H. Erickson. Volume III. Changing children and families*. Rockville, MD: Triangle Press.

Hollander, E., Liebowitz, M., Gorman, J., Cohen, B., Fyer, A., & Klein, D. (1989). Cortisol and sodium lactate-induced panic. *Archives of General Psychiatry*, 46: 135–140.

Kellner, R. (1985). Functional somatic symptoms and hypochondriasis. *Archives of General Psychiatry*, 42:821–833.

Langs, R. (1973). *Psychoanalytic Psychotherapy*, 1. New York: Jason Aronson.

Leckman, J. F., Weissman, M. M., Merikangas, K. R. et al. (1983). Increased risk of depression, alcoholism, panic and phobic disorders in families of depressed probands with panic disorder. *Archives of General Psychiatry*, 40:1055–1060.

Leiberman, J. (1984). Evidence for a biological hypothesis of obsessive-compulsive disorder. *Neuropsychobiology*, 11:14–21.

Levin, S. (1984). Frontal lobe dysfunction in schizophrenia: Impairments of psychological and brain functions. *Journal of Psychiatric Research*, 18:1.

Lewin, K. (1970). *Brief encounters*. St. Louis: Warren H. Green.

Luborsky, L., Singer, B., & Luborsky, L. (1975). Comparative studies of psychotherapies. Is it true that "Everyone has won and all must have prizes?" *Archives of General Psychiatry*, 32:995–1008.

Lurenberg, J., Sivedo, S., Flament, M., Friedland, R., Rapoport, J., & Rapoport, S. (1988). Neuroanatomical abnormalities in obsessive-compulsive disorder detected with quantitative X-ray computed tomography. *American Journal of Psychiatry*, 145:9.

Malcolm, J. (1981). *Psychoanalysis: The impossible profession*. New York: Knopf.

Munoz, R. *Depression prevention research: Toward healthy management of reality*. (1988). San Francisco: Psychiatry Grand Rounds, Langley Porter Neuro-Psychiatric Institute.

Nicholson, R., & Berman, J. (1983), Is follow-up necessary in evaluating psychotherapy? *Psychological Bulletin*, 93:2, 261–278.

NIMH, *Clinical Psychiatric News* (March, 1987). P. 6, Vol. 15. #3.

O'Hanlon, W. (1987). *Taproots*. New York: W. W. Norton.

O'Hanlon, W. & Weiner-Davis, M. (1989). *In search of solutions*. New York: W. W. Norton.

Perls, L. (1977). Two instances of Gestalt therapy. In S. Morce, & R. Watson (Eds.), *Psychotherapies, A comparative casebook*. New York: Holt, Rinehart and Winston.

Perse, T., Greist, J., Jefferson, J., Rosenfeld, R., & Dar., R. (1987). *American Journal of Psychiatry*, 144:12.

Puig-Antich, J. (1986). Biological factors in prepubital major depression. *Pediatric Annals*, 15:12.

Reiss, A., Feinstein, C., & Rosenbaum, K. (1986). Autism and genetic disorder. *Schizophrenia Bulletin*, 12:4.

Rogers, C. (1977). The case of Mary Jane Tilden. In Morse, S., & Watson, R. (Eds), *Psychotherapies, A Comparative Casebook*. New York: Holt, Rinehart and Winston.

Rossi, E., & Cheek, D. (1988). *Mind-body therapy: Methods of ideodynamic healing in hypnosis*. New York: W. W. Norton.

Sagan, C. (1980). *Broca's brain*. New York: Ballantine Books.

Stinchcombe, A., Adams, R., Heimer, C., Scheppele, K., Smith, T., & Taylor, D. (1980). *Crime and punishment: Changing attitudes in America*. San Francisco: Jossey-Bass.

van den Hout, M. Van der Molen, G., Griez, E., Lousberg, H., & Nansen, A. (1987). Reduction of CO2-induced anxiety in patients with panic attacks after repeated CO2 exposure. *American Journal of Psychiatry*, 144:6.

Watkins, J. (1971). The affect bridge: A hypnoanalytic technique: *International Journal of Clinical and Experimental Hypnosis*, 19:1.

Watkins, J., & Watkins, H. (1979) The theory and practice of ego state therapy. In H. Grayson (Ed.), *Short-term Approaches to Psychotherapy*. New York: National Institute for the Psychotherapies and Human Science Press.

Weissman, M. & Boyd, J. (1985). Affective disorders. Epidemiology. In H. Kaplan & B. Saddock, (Eds.), *Comprehensive Textbook of Psychiatry*, (4th Edition). Baltimore: Williams and Wilkins.

Werman, D. (1984). *The Practice of supportive psychotherapy*. New York: Brunner/Mazel.

Woods, S., Charney, D., Goodman, W., & Heninzer, G. (1988). Carbon dioxide-induced anxiety. behavioral, physiologic and biochemical effects of carbon dioxide in patients with panic disorder and in healthy subjects. *Archives of General Psychiatry*, 45:43–52.

Zeig, J. (1980). *A teaching seminar with Milton H. Erickson*. New York: Brunner/Mazel.

Zilbergeld, B. (1989). Personal Communication.

INDEX